PATCHWORK QUILTING WITH WOOL

by

Jean Dubois

Illustrated by Katherine Dubois

DOVER PUBLICATIONS, INC.
NEW YORK

Published in Canada by General Publishing Company, Ltd., 30 Lesmill Road, Don Mills, Toronto, Ontario.
Published in the United Kingdom by Constable and Company, Ltd., 10 Orange Street, London WC2H 7EG.

This Dover edition, first published in 1985, is an unabridged republication of the work first published by La Plata Press, Durango, Colorado, in 1978, under the title *The Wool Quilt: Patterns and Possibilities.* The one photograph that appeared in color in the original edition is reproduced in the Dover edition in black and white (page 67). Foldouts have been converted to double-page spreads.

Manufactured in the United States of America
Dover Publications, Inc., 31 East 2nd Street, Mineola, N.Y. 11501

Library of Congress Cataloging in Publication Data

Dubois, Jean, 1926–
    Patchwork quilting with wool.

    Reprint. Originally published: The wool quilt. Durango, Colo. : La Plata Press, c1978.
    Bibliography: p.
    Includes index.
    1. Quilting—United States—Patterns. 2. Patchwork—United States—Patterns. I. Title.
[TT835.D82 1985]   746.9′7041   84-18860
ISBN 0-486-24821-6 (pbk.)

The value of a revival of any form of art
lies not so much in the emulation of past
achievements as in the fact that, once the
standard of that achievement is recognized
and accepted as a challenge, the artists
evolve a new expression of the art, which has
the further value of being creative, vital,
and contemporaneous.

Cecile de Banke

ACKNOWLEDGEMENTS

Special thanks for the photographs and figures included in this book are due to Leman Publications, Inc.; Old Sturbridge Village; Thomas Crowell, Inc.; the Shelburne Museum, Inc.; the Henry Ford Museum; the Nashville Room of the Public Library of Nashville and Davidson County; the Henry Ford Museum; the Newark Museum; the Mount Vernon Ladies' Association of the Union; the Art Institute of Chicago; the Denver Art Museum; the Philadelphia Museum of Art; and the Royal Ontario Museum.

For photos and/or help and encouragement, I'd also like to thank Barbara Janos and Barbara Ross, Marguerite Wiley, Sally Garoutte, Ava Humble, Peggy Wanamaker, Nancy Crow, Mrs. Thomas B. Johnson, Estelle Diamond, Christine Dubois, Will Dubois, Clara Rogers, Rhea Goldman, Roy Hale, Barbara Todd, Kate and Joel Kopp, Mrs. Forest R. Hall, Harold Miller, Maureen Rastetter, and - last but certainly not least - Edward N. Dubois, the very model of domestic patience.

For advice and help with the photography, special thanks are due to Will Dubois and John Polatty, darkroom wizards of Durango, Colorado; and to Forest R. Hall of Laramie, Wyoming for the design of my photo jig.

Especial and heartfelt thanks go to Kathy Dubois of Milwaukee, Wisconsin, not only for her beautiful illustrations but for general artistic advice and for technical assistance in the drafting of patterns.

TABLE OF CONTENTS

Table of Contents continued

TABLE OF FIGURES

VII

TABLE of PHOTOGRAPHS

PLATE I
Detail, Star (now called Sawtooth Star), worsted, early nineteenth-century New England. This quilt was made from overshot woven wool with a fleur-de-lis figure. The stars are red on a green ground.

Courtesy Old Sturbridge Village

CHAPTER 1

INTRODUCTION

Although my mother pieced the beautiful wool and velvet Windmill Cross quilttop (Plate XIV, Chapter IV) in 1920, it was packed away and neglected until she gave it to me a few years ago. I packed it away myself, then, thinking to save it for one of my daughters. But the more the gas bill went up and the more I lay in bed shivering, nights, thinking about how snug and cozy we used to be at home, sleeping under wool comforters, the more I thought, why don't I get that quilt finished up and use it?

For backing I found a wool-synthetic blend which approximated the soft red which formed the dominant color of the top, and cut it big enough so that it could be turned to the front to form a border which would make the quilt slightly larger. I didn't want a comforter. I'd been looking at pictures of beautiful old wool quilts like the one in Plate I on the facing page, and I wanted my Windmill quilted too.

I'd never done any quilting - thought it was a job for experts - so I asked Mom if she knew of a good professional quilter.

"Wool is never quilted, dear. It's always tied."

"No," I said firmly, "wool quilts are usually tied, to save time. But I'm not in any hurry, I want it quilted."

So we took the top and the backing and the batting to a professional quilter.

"Quilt it? Dear me, no. Wool quilts are always tied, dear," she said.

"Yes," I said firmly, "wool quilts are usually tied, but that's just to save time. I'm not in any hurry, and I'd like it quilted."

"That can't be done, dear. It's too thick to quilt. Wool quilts are always tied." She turned to my mother, who was standing by enjoying my discomfiture. "Aren't they always tied, Mrs. Hall?" Mother allowed as how she'd never seen a wool quilt quilted, and the quilt was tied.

The ties destroyed the design, and I was unhappy with the whole project. I kept thinking about the beautiful colonial wool quilts, and I kept muttering to myself that wool quilts could, too, be quilted. Wool's no thicker than cotton, and has a more open texture; surely the needle would go through wool more easily than through cotton.

Although I had never quilted anything before, I bought a frame and several spools of a soft red mercerized cotton thread, and started quilting Mom's Windmill Cross, as much to show those two darling ladies that wool quilts can be quilted as to rescue a beautiful top from disaster.

In the course of the project, I discovered that quilting is as much fun as patchwork, if not more so. I also discovered the warmth, the glowing colors, and the deep emotional appeal of the wool quilt, and determined to pass that discovery on to all of you.

Knowing nothing at the time about designing quilting patterns, and having no idea how to mark a pattern in any case, I followed the good old American tradition of quilting one-fourth inch in from all the seam lines, and this design proved to be the ideal one to show off the strong geometrics of the pattern. The inadequacies in the quilting lay rather in my difficulties in controlling the length and evenness of the stitch (although my technique improved as I worked) than in any failure of the wool to be quiltable.

Any wool quilt can be tied, of course, and some, like Crazy Quilts, Log Cabins, and the Rocky Road to Kansas, almost invariably are. Tying is faster and easier. If the price of fuel keeps going up faster than we can do our quilting, we may all be tying wool quilts to keep our beds covered, but wool quilts are not tied because they have to be tied. Whether to tie or to quilt is an artistic decision like many another made by the quiltmaker.

Directions for tying a quilt are in Chapter IV, while directions for designing and marking quilting for different kinds of wool quilts are in Chapters II, III, and V.

Wool is making a comeback. Wool blankets are suddenly out-selling the synthetics that have dominated the market for years. Both men's and women's suits are made of wool again, and beautiful displays of wool are being featured in fabric stores. It is not necessary, however, to buy large amounts of wool for quiltmaking. Because of its popularity, wool is showing up on the remnant tables again. Mill ends are available, and of course more and more wool is finding its way into our scrapbags. Wool clothing is usually discarded for reasons of style or boredom long before the usefulness of the material is exhausted. Men's suits, in particular, make good materials for quilts. They are usually of high quality, have interesting, but not obtrusive stripes or plaids. They also come in few color families - blues, greys and blacks, and browns - which go well together so that several suits can be used in the same quilt, providing a background that is interestingly varied but not distractingly so.

I don't know how the myth about wool not being washable got started. Wools are washable, although they shrink and lose their finer qualities when exposed to hot water.

Always wash wools before using them for quiltmaking, whether they are new or recycled. Wool, like other fabrics, is finished with acid, and while this gives it a beautiful surface, many persons are allergic to it, and cannot have unwashed fabric near their skins. Also, once the wool is washed, it is not terribly attractive to moths for some reason, and is softer and easier to quilt. An added advantage of using washed wool for quiltmaking is, of course, that the finished quilt is then also washable.

Before washing, restore clothing to its original pattern pieces. To restore a man's suit, start with the trousers, snipping the stitches that hold the cuff in place. Take out the hems in the bottom of the trousers, and cut off the waistband, cutting around the zipper and the pockets in the process. Now, rip the seams.

The coat is a little harder to deal with. Cut off the buttons and put them in the buttonbox. Cut the sleeves off parallel to the seam, and rip down the underarm seam. Cut the collar and pockets out, and rip along the remaining seams. Wash, dry, and press if necessary. If you cut up each suit as it is discarded, and box the pieces along with others of its color family, getting the materials ready for quiltmaking won't seem like such an overwhelming job when the time comes to start a quilt.

To wash, use Woolite and cold water, washing by hand, or use lukewarm water and ordinary detergent. Rinse well - several times - but never wring. Pat dry in a bath towel, and finish the drying in the dryer, at a delicate setting. Press, if necessary, using the wool setting on the steam iron.

Woolens are best washed in small lots, and because some colors run considerably the first time they're washed, in groups of the same or similar colors. Be cautious about a color which runs; wash it again to see if it's still a bad actor on a second try. If it still runs, find some non-quilt use for it.

Some time before you start making quilts with wool, quilt some experimental squares to check out which types of woolens are best suited to quilting and which to tying. A crisp, hard-surfaced fabric shows off quilting beautifully, while a fleecy or even a soft-surfaced wool will tend to swallow up the stitches and mute the effect.

As I have enjoyed sleeping, toasty-warm, under my wool Windmill, which is now my bedspread, and have worked with wool, making quilts and sample blocks, I have become convinced that the possibilities of the wool quilt are almost infinite. The finished quilts fill a necessary economic and ecological need. They have a subtlety of line and color impossible to achieve with cotton. And they have, in addition, a strong emotional appeal.

In the chapters which follow you'll find a history of the wool quilt in America, along with pictures, patterns and possibilities, diagrams and directions, and the stories of the quilts and the women who made them. There is no way to start at the beginning, with the first quilts made, and proceed on to the most contemporaneous, because all of the quilts - the whole-cloth quilted spread, the framed medallion, the patchwork quilt, the applique quilt, and the pressed quilt - are old, old art forms that came to us from our European ancestors. Each chapter, therefore, begins at the beginning with a different type of quilt, and traces its development up to the present day. It's up to you to carry it over into tomorrow.

PLATE II
Glazed indigo Linsey-woolsey quilted spread made in New England c. 1730.

CHAPTER 2

THE WHOLE-CLOTH QUILTED SPREAD

It is often said that the twentieth-century homemaker has nothing to do, because she has machines for every job. Even with our washing machines and dryers, our dishwashers and vacuum sweepers, our mixers, blenders, juicers, and can openers - even with our specialized machines like hot-dog cookers and spaghetti makers - we still don't have as many machines to help us with our work as the colonial dame had. Much of what most of us do by hand, she did by machine. In addition, the colonial dame was not elected sole housekeeper in her domain. Everyone worked, even the family dog, who often helped with the cooking and churning. If the homemaker did not have a smoke jack or a clock jack or a small boy whose job it was to turn the spit on which the roast was skewered, she trained the dog to walk a treadmill in front of the fireplace. The treadmill, in turn, was rigged to a wheel which kept the roast turning on its spit. The practice was so common that the small, good-natured dogs which usually did this work were called turnspit terriers. Other, larger dogs were trained to walk treadmills which ran the churns.

This is not to downgrade the colonial homemaker; she put in long hours at killing labor. The difference is that she supervised what amounted to a small home industry which routinely produced a great number of products - including yarn, thread, and fabric - which we buy ready-made.

The Production of Linsey-woolsey

The number of machines the colonial dame stored in her home for the production of Linsey-woolsey - the material of which the beautiful old quilts pictured in Plates II, III, and IV were made - staggers the mind. Linsey-woolsey was a loosely-woven fabric made with a linen warp and a woolen weft. It produced a strong, long-wearing, warm, and beautiful cloth much in demand for household use. The earliest quilts made in northeast America, as nearly as we can tell, were made from Linsey-woolsey. Some were worked as whole-cloth quilted spreads; some, made from scraps left over from the making of clothing and other household necessities, were pieced in a variety of patterns, as discussed in Chapters III and IV.

But before Linsey-woolsey could be woven, the wool yarn and the linen thread had to be produced. Linsey-woolsey could be imported, of course, and the beautiful glazed material used for the tops of the quilts in Plates II, III, and IV probably was. But most colonists had little cash. The English mercantile system, which decreed that colonies produce raw materials and consume manufactured

PLATE III
Glazed olive-green Linsey-woolsey quilted spread made in New England c. 1785.

Collections of Greenfield Village and Henry Ford Museum

goods (including textiles) was not particularly meaningful to them, and one of their first efforts when they came to America was to plant flax and to start raising sheep.

It took several years to breed a flock of sheep large enough to produce the wool required to clothe a family, so linen production usually came first. Flax seed was broadcast in May, and by the end of June the crop was ready to harvest. This was work for the men and boys, who pulled the plants up by the roots and laid them out to dry for a day or two, turning them occasionally in the sun. The flax was then rippled in the field with a coarse wooden or heavy iron wire implement with enormous teeth called a ripple-comb. The ripple-comb was fastened to a plank and the flax stalks were pulled through it to break off the seed bolles, which fell onto a sheet to be saved for seed and flaxseed oil.

The stalks were then tied at one end into bundles called beats or bates, and were stacked to dry. Once thoroughly dry, the stalks were retted (rotted) to get rid of the leaves and to make the central core of the plant brittle so that it could be broken and removed. Retting the stalks in ponds was the simplest way, but the decaying flax poisoned fish. On the other side of the Atlantic, steep-pools were staked out in which the bates of flax were piled, each alternate layer at right angles to the one beneath it. A cover of heavy boards and stones was applied, and the flax was kept in water (preferably running water) for four or five days, after which the rotted leaves were removed, and the flax was again dried and tied into bundles. Dew retting, a simpler but more lengthy process scorned by the English, was much used in North America.

Once dried, the hard central core, called the "hexe", had to be removed. This was done by breaking the stalks on a flax-brake, after which they were broken again into smaller pieces on a finer brake. The flax was then scutched with a swingling knife, which was a long wooden instrument with which the flax was beaten with scraping, downward strokes to get the bark off and to remove the broken bits of core. This was hard work, and had to be done twice, but a good swingler could process forty pounds of flax in a day. The flax was then cleaned again, after which it was beetled - i.e., pounded in a wooden trough with an enormous pestle-shaped beetle until it became soft. These were all dusty, dirty, outdoor jobs, usually done by men.

Hackling, which came next, was woman's work, and the dexterity of the hackler was of great importance, because a poor hackler could ruin the best of flax. Hackling is to flax what carding is to wool, and is done on a series of hetchels, each one containing finer teeth than the one before it. The hackler wetted the flax slightly, took ahold of it at one end, and drew it through the hackle teeth toward herself in a way which divided the flax into fine filaments while combing out the short fibres and laying the long ones into continuous threads. When fine linen was required, seven different hetchels were used, after which the fibres were sorted according to their fineness to ready them for spinning.

The flax-wheel, Figure 1, which many modern weavers are using to spin wool by adjusting the tension on the spindle, was invented in the 16th century. In addition to its other advantages, it allowed the spinster to sit at her work. The

Figure 1 - The Flax Wheel in Use -- from *Colonial Living* by Edwin Tunis, The World Publishing Company, 1957.

drive wheel was turned by a crank which was kept going by a treadle. The wheel had two belts. One drove the whorl of the spindle. The other turned the bobbin, which spun freely on the spindle, using it as an axle.

To spin, the spinster arranged the flax on the distaff, put her wheel in motion, and fed the filaments, which she kept slightly damp, into the hollow end of the spindle, where the twisting (which is the process by which filaments become thread) took place. The finished thread then exited through a hole in the side of the spindle and ran through one of the hooks on the horseshoe-shaped "flyer" that was part of the spindle. From the flyer it was wound on the bobbin, which, because of its smaller pulley, ran slightly faster than the spindle.

When the bobbin was full, it was replaced by another, and eventually wound off into "knots" (forty strands) by the use of a hand reel called a niddy-noddy, or a clock-reel, which clicked when forty strands had been wound. There were twenty knots to a skein, and spinning two skeins of linen thread was considered a good day's work.

The skeins now had to be either bleached or dyed, both of which were long and tedious processes, and then they were wound into balls. This required the use of another machine, the swift, which was a favorite lover's gift. A quilling wheel was then used to wind the balls of thread onto spools for the warp and onto quills for the weft before the thread went to the weaver.

Some of these machines may seem unnecessary to those of us whose two hands, held two feet apart and kept in motion, formed a swift for our mothers when their skeins needed to be balls, but it must be remembered that spinning and spool-winding were bottlenecks. An extended family, running what amounted to a home industry, required four spinners to keep one weaver busy.

It was much simpler to make yarn than thread. The sheep were shorn in the spring, and the fleece came to the housewife all in one piece. It was then cleaned and dyed in the wool (i.e., while the fleece was still whole). Wool takes dye well,

Spinning wool yarn

Figure 2 - The Wool Wheel in Use -- from Colonial Living by Edwin Tunis, The World Publishing Company, 1957.

Courtesy Thomas Y. Crowell Company, Inc.

and did not present the problems linen did. Indigo, which could produce a wide range of permanent blue shades, was a great favorite, and was sold by travelling indigo peddlars. Cochineal, also an imported product, produced red, as did madder. The various shades of brown and yellow, and even some purples, generally came from native plants or from garden varieties brought from Europe. Green was a two-step color, involving dyeing blue on top of yellow.

After the cleaning and dyeing, the wool was too dry to handle, so it had to be thoroughly greased, usually with animal fat. It was then ready to be carded. The cards were a set of paddles which had rows of slightly bent wires on one side. The colonial dame, by repeatedly pulling one paddle across the other, eventually managed to fluff the wool and mix it evenly. The end result was a long, narrow, fleecy roll ready to be spun.

The wool wheel (Figure 2) was a far simpler machine than the flax wheel. It was really only a horizontal hand spindle powered by a wheel which was turned by hand. The spinster held the wool in her left hand and manipulated the wheel with a stick held in her right hand. As the turning spindle twisted the wool, she walked backward to keep the proper tension on the yarn. When it got to its optimum length, she quickly stepped forward and, still using the power of the wheel, wound it onto the spindle. When the spindle could hold no more yarn, the spinster stopped her work and wound it off, either by inserting pegs into the spokes of the wheel to form a reel, or by using a niddy-noddy or clock-reel as flax spinsters did. As in flax spinning, forty threads was a knot; but seven knots made a skein. Six skeins of yarn was considered a good day's work, and it has been estimated that a spinster walked twenty miles in a six-skein day, half of it backward.

Many homes had looms, but most villages also had a professional weaver to whom the thread and yarn could be taken to be made into Linsey-woolsey. In any case, the weaving was the fastest of the jobs involved in making a Linsey-woolsey quilt.

Linsey-woolsey Quilts

By the time a top was ready to be marked for quilting, it already represented a large investment of time: the preparation of the flax and the wool, including the dyeing and bleaching; the spinning of the thread and yarn; and the weaving. The homemaker, then, wanted something beautiful for her time and trouble, and the Linsey-woolsey quilted spreads which still exist testify to her success.

Unlike the framed medallion quilts which were being made at the same time in the same families (see Chapter III), these Linsey-woolsey spreads had no strong central focus, but tended, like the East India fabrics so popular among the English-speaking peoples of the 17th century, to exhibit all-over designs interrupted by a strong inner border. These patterns (which were originally drafted from English designs) are still being produced in India and sold as bedspreads and tablecloths. Quilting one of these bedspreads might be a valuable first step in the process of learning to design whole-cloth quilted spreads of the colonial type. If there was a central focus, it tended, like the

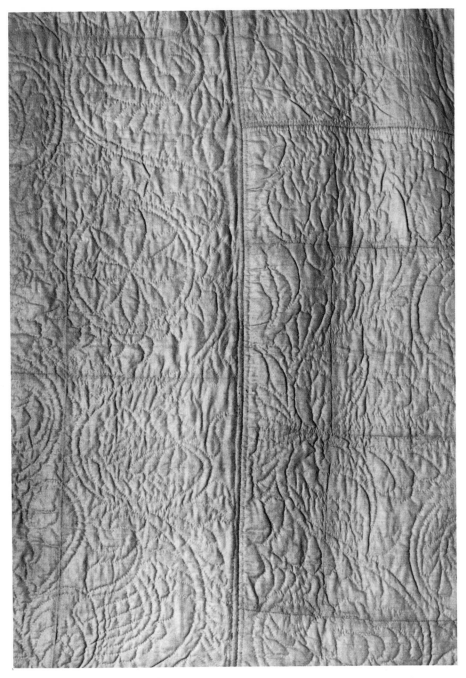

Plate IV
Glazed Linsey-woolsey quilted fragment made by Mrs. Davis in Massachusetts c. 1710-1750.

Collection of the Newark Museum

design of an oriental rug, to be surrounded and somewhat obscured by other motifs, so that the border (or series of borders) even then was the most important design element.

Most of the borders on the Linsey-woolsey quilts were feather borders. Feather quilting - perhaps the favorite of American quilters even now - came from Northumberland, where it had been used as early as 1600. On some quilts, for example on the glazed indigo spread in Plate II, the design was done entirely in giant feather quilting. In others, contrasts to the feathered border were provided by vines, hearts, and flowers, as in Plate III, or even by pineapples, bunches of grapes, and weird and wonderful leaves and tendrils. In most of the Linsey-woolsey quilts, these free-flowing designs were forced into sharp relief by a background of closely set diagonal parallel lines. Usually the parallel stitching runs in from the sides, meeting in a chevron pattern in the center of the quilt, as in Plate II, more clearly shown in Figure 4. Sometimes, however, the parallels went in one direction only on the entire quilt top, as in Plate III.

There was another type of Linsey-woolsey quilted spread, as illustrated by Plate IV, which seems to have been more influenced by the wonderfully free-flowing lines and curves of English crewel embroidery than by the East India prints. This type of quilt is as free from the restraints of the real world as crewel embroidery is. The same vine bears wildly varied blossoms and fruits. Roses, tulips, passion flowers, grapes and pineapples grow happily side by side with the leaves of the oak, the laurel, and the imagination. This type of quilt does not utilize diagonal lines in the background; the quilted designs fill up the entire space.

Linsey-woolsey spreads were enormous. They were meant to go clear to the floor, and sometimes covered several down quilts as well. Although they are called whole-cloth spreads, many, particularly those woven on home looms, are actually made of two or even three lengths of fabric, and sometimes even of smaller pieces of the same color and texture sewed together into a single cloth. The design was often, but certainly not always, worked out with function in mind. Many had the two bottom corners cut out to accommodate the quilt to a four-poster bed. Many had borders around three sides only. The border doesn't go across the top, because that would be behind the pillows and wouldn't show.

Indigo was the most common color. It was dark and did not show dirt, and it was also dependably color-fast. Red, watermelon pink, olive green, apricot, yellow, and cocoa brown were not uncommon. The Shelburne Museum has one which is snowy white and one which is plaid. Glazed woolens were produced in England in stripes and florals as well, and some of these fabrics were undoubtedly made into quilts of this type.

The backing, usually homespun even when the top was an expensive imported glazed Linsey-woolsey, was usually a different color from the front, but the quilting, at least on the best examples, was done in the same color as the top. The edges of the quilt were turned in and sewed together, or bound with a contrasting hand-loomed tape. Not only were these quilts made of warm materials, but they were stuffed with wool as well, sometimes, apparently, in its

Figure 3 - Constructing a Half Running Feather. This was a common Linsey-woolsey outer border.

13

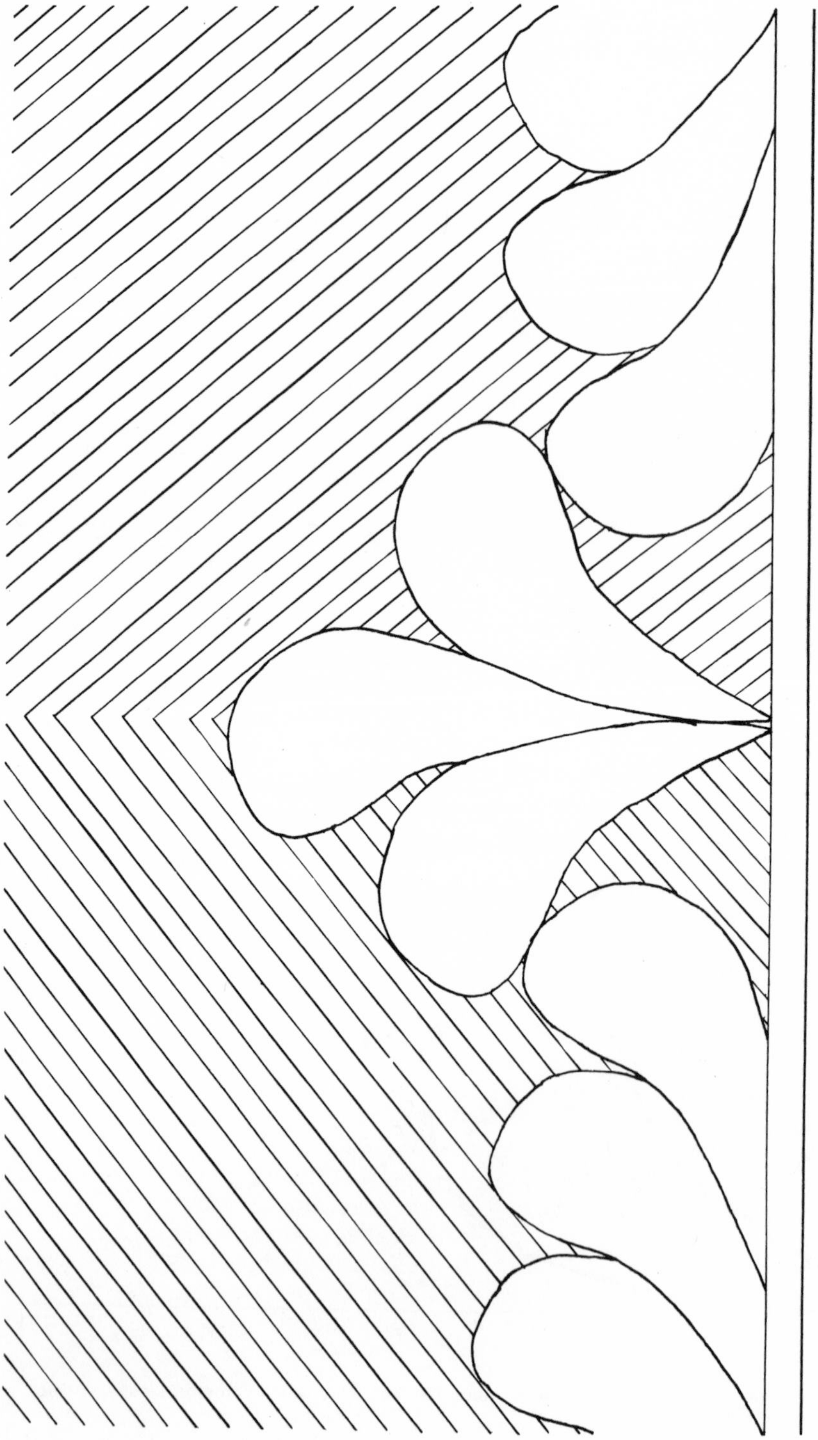

Figure 4 - Midpoint Embellishment, Linsey-woolsey Border.

raw, unwashed state. The Linsey-woolsey quilted spreads of the 17th and 18th centuries were heavy, warm, utilitarian quilts, meant for hard use in a cold climate.

Feather Quilting

Some of the intricate designs typical of the Linsey-woolsey quilts may not be to our taste, and are possibly beyond our competence as quilters. It is often the case, however, that the simplest designs, like the feather quilt in Plate II, are the most effective. Although capable of infinite variety, the feather is easy to manipulate, and fantastic variations in design can be achieved with a steady hand and one feather template.

A common edging on a glazed Linsey-woolsey spread was a half running feather. A line of stitching running parallel to the edge of the quilt formed the spine, and the individual feather segments were marked with a template shaped and notched like the one in Figure 3.

To reproduce this effective border, trace the template in Figure 3 and transfer it to cardboard. Start in the lower lefthand corner, and lay the template so that the point is in the corner and the bottom notch intersects the line of stitching forming the spine. Work to the right, to about the midpoint, placing the template so that the top notch intersects the line of the previous feather and the bottom notch intersects the line of stitching forming the spine. Now, turn the template over, and start in the corner again, placing the template at the same angle to the spine as the first feather you traced. Work to the top of the paper. Now start in the lower righthand corner, and repeat. Plate II shows how the reversed feathers join at midpoint.

Often some sort of an embellishment, as in Figure 4, was used at the midpoint. A more elaborate embellishment can be used, of course - a feathered shell, pineapple, tulip, or heart would be quite in keeping with the Linsey-woolsey spirit and could function to repeat a design element used elsewhere on the quilt.

The midpoint of this border functions in two ways. It makes minor adjustments in spacing possible, thus avoiding the necessity for custom-designing a template which just exactly fits the space. More importantly, it provides a visually exciting way to turn the template around to make the turning of the corners possible. If this border is going to go around all four corners, instead of the traditional three, the template will have to be turned over at each of the midpoints of the quilt rather than simply at the center bottom. In any case, always work from the corners toward the midpoints, and make spacing adjustments at the midpoints. If you are using the three-sided border, you will probably also have to make spacing adjustments at the top. Do this by planning ahead as you approach the top of the quilt, and making each feather segment marginally smaller (or larger) to fit the space.

The template you made for the half-running feather border can be used for a running feather too, of course, by starting out as for a half-border and then

Figure 5 - Constructing a Prince's Plume

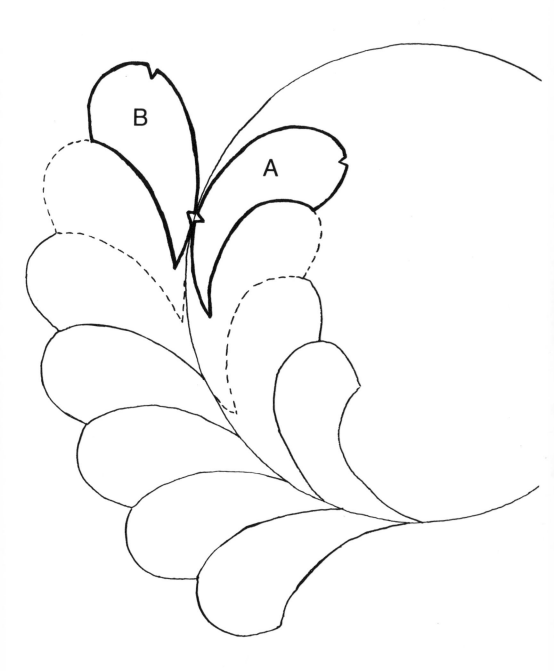

Figure 6 - Constructing a Feather Wreath

17

reversing the template and adding a row of feathers on the opposite side of the spine. It can also be used for a Durham feather or for a meandering feather on any shape curve you wish to design. Draw the spine first and then trace the segments. Start from the bottom and work up, or from the left and work right, placing one notch where the spine and the feather meet and the other where the feather meets the outline of the feather just drawn. When you are ready to do the second side, match notches with the bottom feather on the first side, and try to place the template at about the same angle from the spine as you did on the first side. Practice various curves, and try going around corners with this meandering feather.

This template can also be used for any sort of short curved feather, as in Figure 5. Again, start at the bottom and work up. When you get to the top of your feather, place the template at an attractive angle and trace the top part of it to form a finial.

Feather wreaths can also be made from this same template. However, they are often made with narrower templates, especially in the center, as in Figure 6.

To make a practice feather wreath on paper, using these templates, measure a 2½" radius with your compass, and draw a circle on a piece of paper. Trace templates A and B onto cardboard and cut them out. Do the inside of the circle first, placing template A with its notch on the circle. Match the curve of the circle to the curve of the template as nearly as possible, as in Figure 6. Draw completely around the template. Now, move down and place the template so that the top notch continues the line already drawn across the top of template A and the bottom notch intersects the circle. Draw around the part of the template needed to fill in the feather, as shown by the dotted line in Figure 6. Continue on in a counter-clockwise direction until the circle is complete. As you get down to the last couple of feather segments, you may have to adjust your spacing slightly, so that the last feather is not noticeably larger or smaller than the others. Don't be discouraged if your eraser gets as much use as the business end of your pencil on the first few tries.

Now, take template B and place it below the circle, notch to notch, with the original position of template A, and at the same angle at which it was placed, as in Figure 6. Trace completely around it. Now move template B down. Match one notch with the line coming across the outside edge of the feather above it and place the other notch where it will intersect with the circle. Trace as in Figure 6 (dotted line). Continue on until the circle is complete.

When you have mastered the Durham feather, the meandering feather, and the feather wreath, try reproducing design elements from quilts you admire. Try the feathered hearts, leaves, and flowers from the quilt in Plate III. Practice feathered ovals, and try some of the especially fine feathered corners given in Figures 7, 8, and 9. As with every other feather design, draw the spine first, and then fill in the feather segments along first one side of the feather and then the other, letting the notch on the template make the adjustment to the curve for you. Occasionally, the curve will turn too sharply for the template. On those occasions, use only half the template - either horizontally or vertically - until you

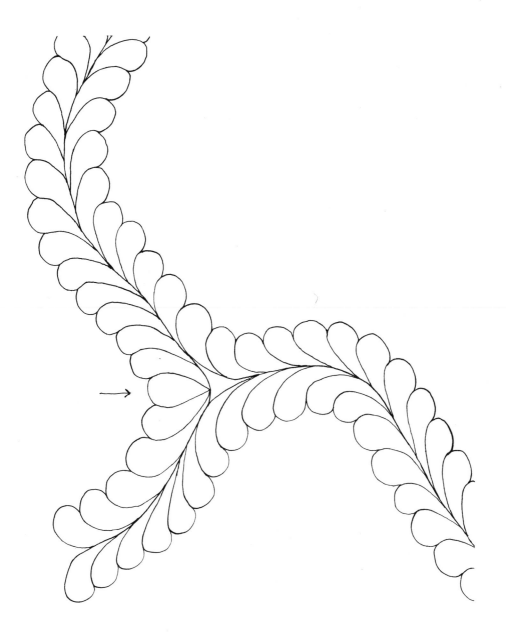

Figure 7 - Corner from a glazed Linsey-woolsey quilt made in New York c. 1800. This is a simple border to make **if** you turn your template over at the sign of the arrow.

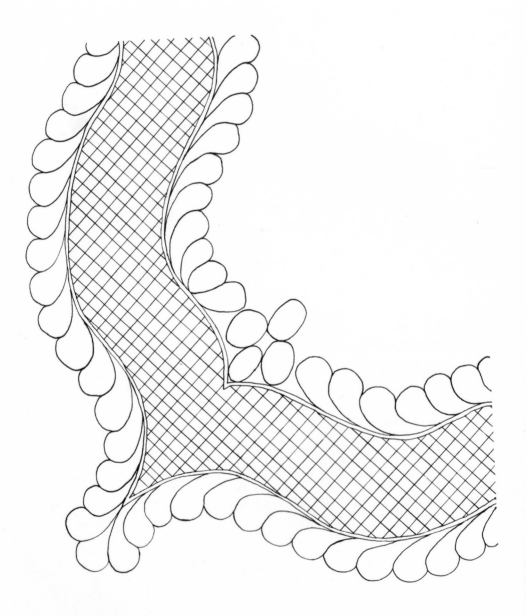

Figure 8 - Corner from the inner border of a glazed Linsey-woolsey quilt made about 1780.

Figure 9 - Corner from the inner border of a glazed Linsey-woolsey quilt made in Massachusetts in 1807. The left-hand meandering feather runs to the top of the quilt, while the right-hand feather leads the eye into the midpoint embellishment of the outer border.

are around the difficult part of the curve. Usually, inside curves give more trouble than outside curves, and oddly enough, the difficulty is encountered as you go into the curve, not while you are in it. Each marker has her own way of adapting to difficulties. Experiment until you find yours.

After you have practiced with these feather templates on scratchpaper, and have learned how to use them, you will want to design your own templates, perhaps flattening them, perhaps making them more curved, so that your feathers will be distinctively your own, rather than mere copies of someone else's idea of a feather. Another way to vary the appearance of the finished design is to move the notches so that the feather stands at a different angle to the circle or the other feathers.

As soon as you are comfortable with these feather techniques on scratch-paper, draft large, quilt-size feather templates (3-3½" long for a single bed, slightly larger for double) and experiment with them, using Magic Marker on old newspapers. This in-scale practice will train your eye to the possibilities of feather quilting, and you will then be only a step away from designing your own whole-cloth feathered quilt.

Now that you know how to use templates, never use a printed pattern again. Let them be an inspiration to you, yes, but don't be a slave to them. Even if your own designs aren't wildly original, their execution will be. Every one of us could use the same template for a running feather border, and come out with a feather that looked slightly different. That is why hand work is so much more satisfying than machine work, and why this quilting revival which started in the late sixties is still booming, and will continue to do so. We are building on what came before; we are not copying. We are trying to reach the standard of what went before, so that we can then continue on to build up a truly personal and contemporaneous art.

Designing the All-quilted Top

Even if you never design a quilt of your own, an understanding of the basic principles of quilt design will add to your enjoyment of the quilts you see in museums, quilt shows, books, and magazines. The function, the size, and the shape of the quilt are the determining factors of the design. It is a space to be filled, and because one of the purposes of the quilting is to hold the top, lining, and batting firmly together, it has to be filled without leaving large, unstitched spaces.

Some sort of organization is necessary. A bold center motif and a series of borders is a common one, especially in England and Wales, but by no means the only one, as balance can be achieved in many other ways.

Contrast is essential, and is commonly achieved by setting off geometrics with curved lines, or vice versa, but this is not the only way to achieve contrast. Differences in size provide as effective a contrast as differences in shape. The contrast is often provided by the background, as in the early American Linsey-woolsey quilts, where the close-set diagonal lines provide a contrast to the large feather motifs in both size and shape. The double function of the background is one of the reasons these Linsey-woolsey quilts are so effective. A small-scale wineglass or shell background, of course, works as effectively for a bold, straight-line design.

It is fairly easy to design the quilting pattern for a patchwork or applique top. The design statement has already been made. It is simply a matter of discovering a quilting pattern which fits into the physical space allotted to it, and which re-enforces the statement already made, or at least does not contradict it. It is another thing altogether to design a pattern for an all-quilted top, and you should study good examples before you begin. This is not to say, however, that you should copy someone else's work. Quilting has survived as a satisfying art form through countless generations not only because it is a useful craft, but because it is a satisfying one-of-a-kind art which provides each artist the thrill of creativity each time she makes a quilt.

Even though it is difficult, there is nothing arcane about designing a quilt. Quilt design is simply a series of artistic decisions. The first decision to be made is one of function. For what purpose are you designing this quilt? If for competition or for hanging on a wall, a rectangular, symmetrical design is extremely popular, but in this kind of a quilt your idea, or artistic statement, can be expressed in any size or shape. If you wish to work in a traditional vein, check Averil Colby's **Quilting** out of the library, and study the excellent photographs of English and Welsh quilts presented there.

If the quilt is intended to be a bed quilt, we have a much harder problem. We do not necessarily need symmetry, but we must achieve a satisfying balance. If the quilt is to be used on a bed, probably it will be bordered on three sides only, as the top is hidden behind the pillows, and the effectiveness of an all-around border is destroyed the moment the quilt is put on the bed. It may also be shaped differently from a wall quilt. You may want to shape it to fit the bed more gracefully. Historically, squares were cut out of the lower-left and lower-right corners, to accommodate the four-poster beds of the time. Modern workers, particularly when they are designing quilts that will hang to the floor, often curve the two bottom corners, so that the quilt hangs exactly to the floor all the way around.

A single-bed quilt is not merely a smaller double-bed quilt; it is entirely different in shape as well as in size. Queen-size quilts are almost square. In addition to requiring a differently shaped design, the larger quilts require larger-scale patterns than the smaller ones, and can be more elaborate.

Our first step, then, is to decide on the function of the quilt, its size and shape. We should then also remind ourselves that, on our first time out, we ought not to try to be too fancy. Hall and Kretsinger picture a most effective feather quilt (Plate CXIII, p. 250) consisting only of a central feathered oval surrounded by a meandering feather inner border backed by a square diamond filling.

However simple or however elaborate, decide first on your central design. If you are designing a wall quilt, the size of this central medallion will be determined by your personal taste; if for a bed quilt it should be about the size of the top of the bed. Work out your idea on scratchpaper, adjusting it to the shape it is going to have to occupy. Next, work out your outer border, paying especial attention to the corners, and solving your spacing problems at midpoint. Is a central medallion, fenced in by a border, and combined with a contrasting background (still to be chosen), going to be sufficient, or do you need a meandering feather or some secondary motif between the border and the central medallion?

Visualizing how a quilt will look on a bed, hanging down from the sides and adjusting to the curve of the pillows, is much more difficult than visualizing it flat. The problem can be solved, however, by designing the quilt on the bed. Decide on the size your finished quilt will be, make a paper quilt out of taped-together newspapers and lay it on the bed. If it is a floor-length quilt, decide whether or not you want to round the corners, and if so, cut them.

In general, the central motif should cover the top of the bed, or very nearly so, visually if not actually. A twin bed presents a vastly different design problem than a double bed, and if you design your quilt on the bed, you will never fall into the error of designing a central medallion which is the wrong size and shape for the bed. Even with a twin bed, however, it is important to think BIG. Look again at Plate II, to see the scale of the feather being used there.

Make a number of sketches first, using the dimensions of the bed in miniature. Then try out the design in your mind's eye, deciding where each motif should be placed on the bed. Mark the edges of the bed on the newspaper "quilt", and remove it to a table top. Remembering where you decided each design motif should be, start marking with a Magic Marker, using the templates you designed while still in the practice stage. It is not necessary to use several different templates, however. A perfectly beautiful feather quilt can be designed with only one template.

Do the central bed-top design first. Then do the outer border. Then fill in the rest of the design, leaving the background until last.

Put the finished newspaper quilt back on the bed and see how it is going to look. Study it to see if each motif is placed where it is visually most satisfying. Maybe it needs to be moved; maybe it needs to be made slightly larger or slightly smaller. Check the placement of borders, of meandering feathers. Do they need to be closer to the center, or farther away? Are they on the right scale? It is hard, at first, to think big enough, and when designing your first quilt, you may have to do two newspaper designs. Later on, you'll get it the way you want it on the first try. Still later, you'll find that you have to newspaper-mark only half the design to assure yourself that your sketch will work.

Marking the Quilt-top

Once you are satisfied with the newspaper design, cut your quilt top to the same size as your newspaper "quilt". Measure and mark off, with dressmaker's chalk, a vertical line down the center, a horizontal one across the center, and a rectangle representing the top of the bed, before you begin to mark your design. Now begin to mark, using dressmaker's chalk.

When marking, remember that the placement of the patterns has to be exactly measured. The central motif must be in the center. The border must be the same width all around the quilt. If the design is symmetrical, the identical motifs have to be placed in **exactly** opposite positions on the quilt top.

Mark the center first. The central motif should be in the exact center of the quilt if it is to be a framed-medallion hanging quilt, but for a bed quilt it must be in the visual center. That is sometimes quite a different thing. After the center has been marked, mark your outer border, starting in the corners and working toward midpoint, making minor space adjustments there if necessary. Then mark in inner borders, or intermediate design elements.

Once the major design elements have been measured and marked, you don't need to be such a martinet about measuring. Minor variations in filling in details is natural, and even effective, as it emphasizes the individuality of the quilter, and differentiates the work from machine quilting and kit-work.

Mark in your background last, choosing it for simplicity and contrast. The marking of the background patterns must be perfectly done. Minor flaws, such as parallel lines which are not parallel, or lines which do not take up at exactly the same place after being interrupted by another pattern, can ruin a beautiful design. If you are using a diamond or a square in the background, mark it as you would parallel lines, doing all the parallels in one direction before coming back and marking the opposite direction. Be certain that these lines continue on in exactly the same direction after being interrupted by a pattern.

It is impossible to emphasize too strongly the fact that background lines, either parallel or cross-hatch, must be absolutely straight and always absolutely the same distance apart. An easy solution is to use a yardstick, marking on both sides of it and using its width to determine how far apart your lines will be. If its width turns out not to be appropriate, find another long, sturdy, straight board which is the width your pattern demands. Engineering supply houses carry ruled plastic straight-edges which are handy, because you can see through them, and line up your edge with the line just drawn. This is far more practical than trying to measure each of hundreds of lines. You will find, in working with large feathers, that the one-inch width represented by the typical yardstick is too wide; you will probably need the greater contrast provided by lines that are a half-inch to three-quarters of an inch apart.

Other Whole-cloth Quilted Spreads

The manufacture of glazed Linsey-woolsey was the last attempt of the English woolen mills to compete with cotton, and glazed Linsey-woolsey gradually became unavailable. Whole-cloth wool quilts continued to be made, however, even though glazed wool was no longer available. The Amish, who came to Pennsylvania in 1727, possibly either brought with them or adopted fairly quickly, beautiful whole-cloth quilting designs that are still being made in a few conservative communities.

I have not been able to find any 18th-century examples of Amish whole-cloth quilts, but the fact that several conservative 19th-century bishops in the midwest forbade patchwork as frivolous, yet condoned the whole-cloth quilts, indicates that the whole-cloth quilt was a step back rather than a step forward. The twentieth-century whole-cloth quilts made in these communities do not present an essentially different appearance from the backs of the Amish framed medallion quilts discussed in Chapter III, any one of which can form a model for a beautiful whole-cloth quilted counterpane. This may be because, even though having given up their "worldly" patchwork, Amishwomen clung to their traditional quilting patterns, which were designed to fit into the patchwork. Exceptions are all-over patterns which cover the entire surface except for an outer border, usually a cable. These quilts may be a reversion to an older tradition kept alive, or they may simply be an obvious solution to the artistic problem presented, just as the similar East India designs are.

The shiny-surfaced whole-cloth quilt was too beautiful to disappear with Linsey-woolsey, and it has continued to be made until this day, sometimes of satin, sometimes of cotton sateen. Originally, it was still interlined with wool, as its predecessor was, but gradually it evolved into two types. Some became bedspreads, like the beautiful Rose Quilt in Plate V. Others, keeping the thickness of the original, became the slippery, machine-quilted satin comforters that caused many of us such difficulties in our youth. I am sure I am not the only one who, waking up shivering in the middle of the night, picked the "comforter" up off the floor for the umpteenth time, and safety-pinned it to the sheet for greater security.

Since quilting has tended to be subservient to pieced work in this country, there were few women who could design and mark a whole-cloth quilted spread, and the tops, at least in this century, were usually sold already marked. The Rose Quilt pictured in Plate V was probably commercially marked, and is typical of the best of these commercial designs. It reflects the simplicity and openness of the American taste, as opposed to the more ornate designs in use for the previous two hundred years in England and Wales.

Close inspection of Plate V reveals the basic simplicity of the design. The border is formed by the repetition, twice in each corner, of a rose and tendril pattern (Figure 10). A smaller rose motif (Figure 11) is inserted between them at each corner. A similar rose motif, which can be seen to be the basic rose from the other two motifs, turned upsidedown and provided with graceful, outward-spreading tendrils, serves as a midpoint embellishment center top and center bottom. The left and right midpoints need a larger embellishment because of the greater space involved, and this need is filled by reversing the rose motif used in the corners.

The central medallion is made up of this same rose and tendril motif, except that on one side the terminal triangular tendril has been modified into a curved tendril like those across the top of the design. Two of these motifs are then reversed when the rose and tendril is combined into a diamond for the central

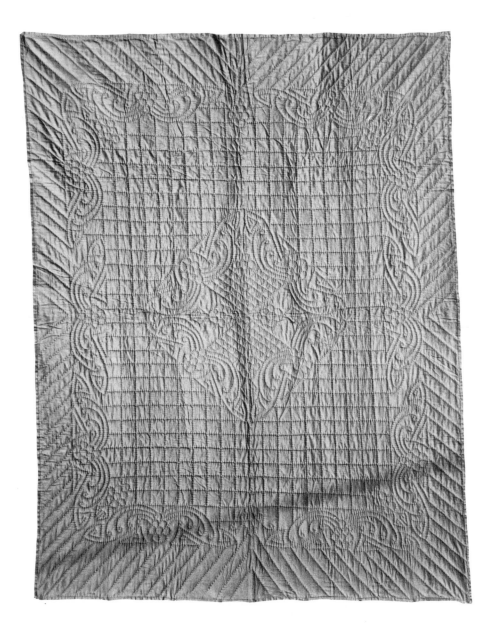

PLATE V
The Rose Quilt, made by Myrtle Hersch in Pagosa Springs, Colorado, about 1918. Both top and backing are rose sateen, and the quilting is done in heavy embroidery floss.

Courtesy Marguerite Wiley, Pagosa Springs, Colorado

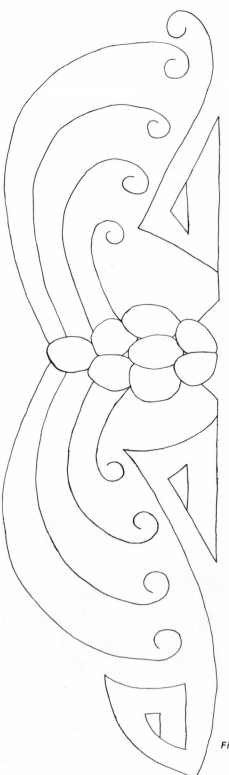

Figure 10 - Rose and Tendril Motif from
the Rose Quilt in PLATE V.

Figure 11 - Rose Corner Motif from the
Rose Quilt in PLATE V.

medallion, so that the four remaining terminal triangles meet at the top and the bottom of the diamond. The small rose motif from the corners is then inserted top, bottom, and both sides (see Plate V), and the interior space is divided into triangles, two of which are cross-hatched into small hanging diamonds which provide a straight-line contrast to the curved lines of the basic design. The background, also providing straight-line contrast, is done in simple squares inside the border, while the outer border is done in parallel lines which come together chevron-like at the midpoints.

The Rose Quilt is a good example of what a sophisticated sense of design can do with one major motif and two minor, closely related ones, and could easily serve as your model for designing original whole-cloth woolen spreads.

PLATE VI
Detail, the Penn Treaty Quilt, cotton and linen, said to have been made by Martha
Washington. This quilt is typical of the best framed medallions being made at the time
in England and in America.

CHAPTER 3

THE FRAMED MEDALLION

Another quilt model which the English settlers brought with them, and which was being made in the same families at the same time as the Linsey-woolsey quilts, was the framed medallion. The framed medallion quilt has a strong central motif surrounded by a multiplicity of patchwork and applique borders of various widths, some of which sometimes repeat the central motif in their corners. The general effect is often one of inutterable clutter, particularly to the American eye, and framed medallions fell from favor in this country by the end of the 18th century, not to be revived until recently.

Martha Washington's Quilt

The quilt in Plate VI illustrates the central section of a quilt said to have been made by Martha Washington and given to her niece, Frances Dandridge Lear, in whose family it remained until it was given to the Mount Vernon Ladies' Association of the Union in 1931. It is a fine example of this type of quilt and one which was typical of the best of the framed medallions being made at that time on both sides of the Atlantic. Its central panel is a scene of Penn concluding his treaty with the Indians, an English copper-plate printed cotton known to have been available in Philadelphia in the 1780's. It is surrounded by a variety of patchwork and appliqued borders made from printed linens and cottons. It measures approximately 100 inches square and by its tasteful balance of elements represents the best of its kind.

Martha Washington

Martha Dandridge Custis Washington (Plate VII) grew up in Chestnut Grove, a plantation in the tobacco country near Williamsburg, Virginia, the eldest of eight children. At 16, she was a tiny girl with brown hair and shining, flirtatious eyes in a rather plain face. Her popularity in Williamsburg society was firmly based on her ability to be pleasantly flattering to both sexes and all ages.

In 1749, when she was 18, she married Captain Daniel Parke Custis, an extremely rich man more than twice her age. They settled at the White House, a tobacco plantation on the Pamunkey. It was a happy marriage and they had four children, only two of whom, Jack and Patsy, survived babyhood.

Custis died of a heart attack in 1757 when Jack was five and Patsy was three. Since Custis, a comparatively young man, had left no will, Martha shared the estate equally with her two children.

Soon afterward, Martha met George Washington. Home on leave to recover from a bout of dysentery, he was at the height of his reputation as a frontier soldier. They became engaged before he went back to the frontier. In 1759, when Washington got his next leave, Martha powdered her hair and looped it with pearls to set off her yellow brocade dress, and married him. Both, as was the custom of wealthy Virginia landowners, considered the marriage a social step and a business arrangement, but this marriage also seems to have been serenely happy.

With the help of Martha's money, George developed Mount Vernon into a complete farm community of some 8,000 acres and 250 persons, self-contained and self-supporting, with its own shops, mills, docks and ships on the Potomac. Martha supervised the kitchens, storehouses, weaving house, gardens, and the housekeeping, as well as seeing after the health, welfare, and training of the negro slaves. She was a good manager, and although Mount Vernon was a prosperous plantation, nothing was wasted under her supervision. It is told of Martha Washington that she always had all her worn silk gowns dyed and ravelled with care so that the thread could be wound on bobbins to be woven into chair and cushion covers. These in turn were not thrown out when worn spots appeared. She once displayed a dress to visitors which was made of material in which white cotton stripes alternated with red silk stripes recycled from chair covers and the General's worn-out stockings.

The management of Mount Vernon, then, was no easy thing. Every day Martha worked from dawn until about three o'clock. She then changed into formal dress and devoted the rest of the day to her husband and children, to her frequent guests, and to reading and dining.

She was an indulgent mother, so fearful of her children's health (she had lost two, and her remaining daughter, Patsy, was an epileptic) that George once had to make a secret appointment with a doctor in Baltimore to get Jack vaccinated, because Martha couldn't stand the worry of it. She never went visiting, although that was the custom of Virginia society, because she did not want to leave the children. She spoiled them outrageously, and, although George was devoted to them and concerned for their welfare, he could do little with them as they grew older, particularly as they were millionaires in their own right.

Martha's daughter Patsy died at seventeen, and after that, as Martha and George had no children of their own, Martha tried to fill that void in her life with the companionship of a succession of young girls growing up in the family.

Martha spent every winter of the revolution in the Continental camp with her husband. As soon as the army went into winter camp, and it was safe for her to come, Martha took the long trip up the rutted roads of the eastern seaboard to join him, bringing what groceries and supplies the family coach could carry. She stayed as long as possible - usually about six months - passing her time with the other officer's wives in mending for their husbands and the bachelor officers, and in making bandages for the hospital. Undoubtedly they made quilts as well. Although the life was isolated and comfortless, she made the best of it in a discreet and good-humored way, and often expressed a low opinion indeed of the

PLATE VII
Martha Washington, miniature painted by Charles Willson Peale in 1776.

officer's wives who did not come to share the winter with their husbands.

George got home to Mount Vernon only once during the Revolution, when, in 1781, he passed by on the way to the seige of Yorktown. At that time Martha entertained his staff and the French commander, the Comte de Rochambeau, and his staff at Mount Vernon. Evidently her son, Jack Custis, who up to that time had been content to stay at home with his wife and children, was inspired by the pomp and glitter, for he promptly signed on as a civilian aide. It was a fatal decision; he died of typhus soon afterward.

When Jack's widow remarried, George suggested that the two youngest Custis children come to Mount Vernon to live. Martha was pleased and grateful for this second family, and was far less indulgent with them than she had been with her own children.

For many years, as the General's wife, Martha had accepted every politeness or attention she got as a tribute to George, and not to her. She was amazed, then, when she arrived in New York a month after the inauguration, to discover that she was now a public person in her own right. She was saluted by cannon. Officials bowed and scraped. Crowds cheered and stared.

The official household she ran for the President, first in New York and then in Philadelphia, was large. Five secretaries took care of George's correspondence and her social calendar. Servants were needed to take care of the guests, to provide the food and to serve the dinners. A few were slaves from Mount Vernon, but most were whites engaged locally.

The Washingtons kept a fashionable house, furnished in the best of taste, said to be decorous as a church. A touch of elegance was provided by the powdered footmen, dressed in the Washington scarlet and white livery. All the while he was president, Washington held weekly levees at which gentlemen had an opportunity to bow to him and to say a few words. Martha held weekly "drawing rooms", at which she sat ensconced on the sofa to receive the ladies' curtsies and the gentlemen's bows while George circulated politely among the guests, making sure he greeted every one of them. They also held weekly official dinners, which were known as formidable occasions. Martha, at that time of her life a plump, neat little woman with white hair under a high-crowned cap, was greatly admired for her unassuming manners and for her sweetness, but she was admitted to be no manager of intellectual entertainment. The old soldier, on the other hand, was the most courteous listener in the world, but he had never mastered the art of conversation. Official dinners were known for their delicious food and almost unendurable silences.

Martha summed up her attitude to her job as First Lady - and indeed to life as well - in a letter she wrote to Mercy Warren soon after she became First Lady: "I sometimes think the arrangement is not quite as it ought to have been; that I, who had much rather be at home, should occupy a place with which a great many younger and gayer women would be prodigiously pleased...I know too much of public life. I am still determined to be cheerful and to be happy in whatever situation I may be; for I have also learned from experience that the greater part of

PLATE VIII
Typical Welsh Quilt, c. 1880. Note particularly the excellence of the design of the quilting, especially in the central medallion.

our happiness or misery depends upon our dispositions, and not upon our circumstances."

By 1797, at the end of Washington's second term, Martha had become a delicate old lady and her family coddled her. A working housekeeper took over the household management, and her grand-daughter, Nelly Custis, helped with the social duties. Even so, she outlasted George, who caught cold while riding his estate in December of 1799. Martha woke in the middle of the night, and, frightened by his struggle to breathe, started to get up to go for help. George refused to let her go. It would be folly for her, considering her susceptibility to colds, to get out of the bed in the bitter cold room, he told her. Wait until the maid comes to make up the fire. No one ever disobeyed George Washington, and Martha lay beside him, waiting, frightened and frantic, for some three hours until the maid came.

It was Washington's last day. His physicians did everything they could: bleeding, blistering, and poulticing, in the hope of relieving his inflamed throat. In the end, Martha stood looking down on the big, quiet man, and said that it was well that the struggle was over, and that she would follow him soon.

Martha lived until May of 1802, a respected great lady, attended by her granddaughter Nelly, who, with her husband, stayed with Martha at Mount Vernon as long as she lived.

Welsh Framed Medallions

The Welsh interpretation of the framed medallion was similar in basic construction to the English and American quilts exemplified by the Martha Washington quilt, but it provided a quiet surface intended to display the quilting. The beautiful quilt in Plate VIII is a typical Welsh framed medallion, and has an almost contemporary look to it even though it is a hundred years old. It was among the quilts displayed in Denver in 1976 in the "British Quilts 1820-1975" exhibition sponsored by the British Council and Bonnie Leman, the Editor of the **Quilter's Newsletter Magazine**, for the purpose of tracing English influences on American quiltmaking, and of illustrating the exchange of ideas between English and American quiltmakers.

This quilt is made up in pink, lavender, purple, and tan cottons and, unlike the Amish quilts which it so closely resembles, makes use of three different prints.

Wool Batting

This Welsh quilt, like many English quilts of its period (and since), has a wool batting, which gives it an almost unbelievable softness. Most quilt historians dismiss the wool batting as unimportant in American quilts, pointing out the difficulties of working with wool; the relatively poor quality of American wool in the early days; and the easy availability of cotton and cotton batts. I think it likely, however, that wool was much used in utility quilts, which being worn out and gone, are not represented in museum collections and have therefore not crossed the consciousness of quilt historians. Wool was readily available. In spite of the difficulties of working with it, women everywhere were managing to clean it, card it, spin and weave with it, and there is no reason to think that the less desirable parts of the fleece - the forelegs and underbelly - which were difficult to spin, were not utilized in quilts. I think the insistence that American women found wool too difficult to handle is based on a gross underestimation of the role women played in the taming of the wilderness.

Doris Hale, writing in the **Better Homes and Gardens** of April 1934, still recommended wool as the warmest interlining and the best for showing off the beauty of the quilting pattern, while at the same time tentatively crediting the development of the glazed-surface cotton batt in the 1920's with giving impetus to the great quilt revival of the 1920's and 30's by simplifying the most tedious part of quiltmaking. And preparing and installing the batting was - and is - a tedious process if done from scratch.

A good batting has to have more virtues than meet the eye. It must be soft, warm, easy to sew through. It must be washable, and it must not shrink when washed. It must be of uniform thickness, capable of being handled without tearing or pulling thin in places. It must be thick enough and firm enough to show off the quilting.

The quilting is given its character by the padding, so the choice of a batt is an artistic as well as a functional one. Wool, of course, is the warmest and the softest, and makes possible the most beautiful and lasting quilting designs. Historically, it has been difficult to work with, however. It has to be cleaned, carded, and laid on the batt evenly. There is some disagreement about how much cleaning is necessary and desirable. For some uses - as in armor, where part of its function was to be impenetrable, it was not cleaned at all, but was soaked in vinegar instead. This was ostensibly to give it more body, and to protect the wool from moths, but may also have been a borrowing from Roman custom. The Romans assigned supernatural healing powers to wool, and wool dipped in oil and wine or vinegar was the recommended remedy for many ailments and disabilities incurred by soldiers, especially dislocations and aching sinews.

Although some early Linsey-woolsey quilts have a thin layer of unwashed wool as a filling, most quiltmakers avoided the use of unwashed wool. It stained the top with oil and it had an unpleasant odor when warm or wet. So most quiltmakers scoured their wool in soapy water, leaving only enough oil in it to make it manageable when it was being carded. It then had to be rinsed a number of times, and dried in the sun. Carding, which removed burrs and tangles, also mixed the wool, and in the end produced a fluffy roll of even thickness. In the rural districts and out on the frontier, carding was done by hand with a pair of paddles fitted with bent nails, and was a tedious process, but in the more settled districts it was possible to have the cleaned wool carded by machine. It was then necessary to spread it evenly on the quilt backing, and this was more difficult with wool than with cotton, because wool is so springy that it cannot be stretched without pulling it thin in places.

Cotton was difficult to work with too, of course, particularly before the invention of the cotton gin. But many quiltmakers felt it was cleaner. It did not have to be protected from moths. It was cheap and readily available. When cotton batting began to be manufactured commercially in this country about 1850, it soon became the standard batting. For many years it was sold only in rolls which opened out into strips about a yard wide. You all know from your own experiences with the unglazed cotton batting still available, just how difficult it was to get the roll open and evenly spread on the quilt backing. It had to be crossed and criss-crossed to get an even thickness, and little scraps had to be stuck in here and there where the cotton was a little thin.

It was not until about 1928 that modern batting with a glazed surface took the complicated business of putting a quilt into the frame out of the hands of experts and within the reach of anyone who was minded to try it.

Synthetic materials, which are glazed and even easier to work with, are now gradually taking the place of the natural fibres on both sides of the Atlantic. They do not "bunch" with age; they are reasonably cheap and easy to quilt through; two or three layers can be used for extra warmth or puffiness; and they wash and dry easily and quickly. There is no comparison, however, in the softness of the finished quilt and in the pure sensual pleasure of working with natural fibres, and most women whose chief interest in quiltmaking is in the quilting itself have stuck with wool and cotton.

Wool, which gives the most beautiful results to the quilter, does have disadvantages. It is easily damaged by being washed in hot water. It is the most expensive of the available battings. It must be protected from moths. If you decide to use wool, it is important to purchase a batt which is exactly the right size, since wool is so springy that it cannot be stretched without tearing thin in places. Therefore, it might be a good idea when designing a quilt which is to have a wool batt to buy the batt first and size the quilt accordingly.

Wool batts, either plain or covered with cheesecloth for greater ease of handling, are available now from the Rastetter Woolen Mill in Millersburg, Ohio* in the following sizes: 42 x 60; 60 x 90; 72 x 90; 80 x 90; and 90 x 96. They will also recycle old battings, and wash, pick, and card raw wool.

The mill, formerly the R. V. Aling Wool Mill, has been in the family for over a hundred years, and the present owners, Maureen and Tim Rastetter, are the third generation to provide wool batts, blankets, and comforters. Their carding machine, a great tourist attraction, is 115 years old, and is probably the oldest operating carding machine in the United States.

Amish Framed Medallions

The framed medallion was not really a wool quilt until it got into the hands of the Amish, an Anabaptist sect which settled in Lancaster County, Pennsylvania, in 1727. Because the Amish shun the world around them, clinging to their own Pennsylvania Dutch dialect, an austere religion, and a simple rural way of life among their own kind, their life today is much as it was when they first came to

* Rastetter Woolen Mill, Route 62, Millersburg, Ohio 44654

these shores in search of religious freedom. It is surely one of the ironies of history that the New World passion for space and simplicity has found its highest expression (quilt-wise) among a community which has turned its back so determinedly on American society and has clung so tenaciously to its Old-world values.

In Amish hands, the framed medallion has been reduced to its barest essentials - stark, geometric designs composed only of squares, rectangles, and triangles worked in a palette of glowing wools, and embellished with elaborate and exquisitely worked quilting. Although the popularity and emotional appeal of the Amish quilts depend almost equally on their color and workmanship as on their design, we should ignore the color for a moment so that we can give our entire attention to the basic simplicity of the design. Assuming that the original Amish quilt was a whole-cloth quilted spread, and that the framed medallion arose from a need to make better use of remnants and recycled clothing, the drawings in Figure 12 (all taken from antique Amish quilts) show what might have been a logical development: first a wide border around the outside; second the greater excitement generated by also inserting the darker material as an inner border; third an elaboration of the inner border into an even more exciting statement. The fourth quilt in Figure 12 probably came about as a combination of the design ideas in 12-a and 12-b; it keeps both the outer and inner borders. Squares of the inner material in the corners of both borders were undoubtedly used as a means of unifying the whole, a solution which is even more effective in color than it is in black and white.

Figure 13 shows an Amish favorite, the Bars design, as it has appeared in antique quilts, showing its elaboration from a simple beginning which probably had its origin in the necessity to find a way to combine remnants of two colors, while also fulfilling the artistic needs of its creator.

The basic square within a square, called Diamond in a Square (Figure 14-a), probably developed from the design in Figure 12-a, either from the necessity to enlarge the central square before framing it, or from an innate urge to create a more exciting pattern. The other quilts in Figure 14 show the same kind of development as that in Figures 12 and 13: an elaboration; an experimentation; a development within a tightly controlled form.

We have in these quilts all the elements of the English framed medallion - and more. Yet, only partly because no prints are used, we have no feeling of clutter, no feeling of being restricted by the demands of the form. The Amish framed medallion is, as you can see by the few variations shown here, capable of infinite variety. At the same time, it holds the actual work of construction to a minimum. In contrast to a pieced quilt top, which can take months to construct, an Amish framed medallion quilt top can be put together in a few hours. Even though the Amish do not gladly accept machinery, Amish women do use treadle sewing machines, and the tops of the framed medallions are always machine-made, although the quilting is always done by hand.

While I am not suggesting a slavish copying of Amish design, I do recommend a close study of it, and a careful consideration of the Amish

a   The Framed Square

b   The Inner Border

c   The Double Inner Border

d   Combination of (a) and (b), with the addition of square insets.

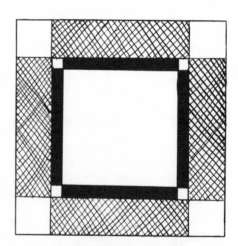

Figure 12 - Variations of the Basic Amish Framed Medallion

approach. These basic Amish designs - the framed square, the inner border and the double inner border; Bars; and the Diamond in the Square - represent high style in the American utility quilt. They are quickly made; they are warm and serviceable; they are beautiful; they are easily adapted to any size and shape of bed; and they present the opportunity to use materials at hand in an interesting and effective way.

a   Bars and Border

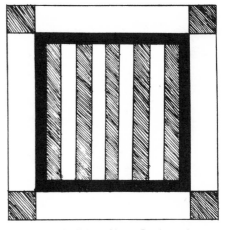

b   Addition of Inner Border and
     Square Inserts in Outer Border

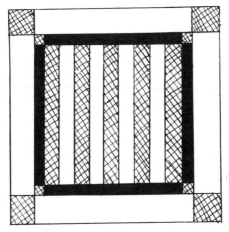

c   Addition of Square Inserts in Inner Border

Figure 13 - Variations of the Amish Bars Quilt

The color of Amish quilts is distinctly their own and may not present the inspiration and opportunity to us that their design does. Although the Amish women live what might seem outwardly drab lives, they have a deep appreciation of color, and many have a sure instinct for its effective use. Black is much used (in contrast to other American quilts, which traditionally reserved its use for mourning quilts) not only for emphasis and contrast to the blazing beauty of their other colors, but because it is much used in their outer clothing. Their dresses and aprons, however, both cotton and wool (and of late years, wool-like synthetics) provide the mauves, lavenders, purples, pinks, cranberries, maroons, emeralds, and blues which for generations they have been combining in dramatic ways, unique until the advent of modern graphics.

41

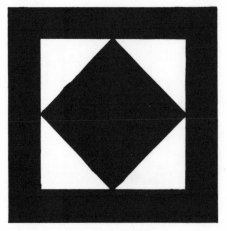

a   Simple solids

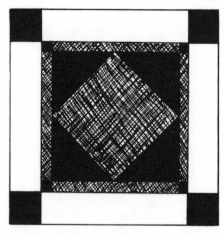

b   Addition of inner border and of
     square inserts in borders

c   Addition of additional inner border

d   Simplification of (c)

Figure 14 - Variations of the Amish Diamond in a Square

It is easy to slip from the bold to the garish, however, and not all Amish color schemes are equally successful, although the current popularity of everything Amish tends to blind us to that fact. Wool, because of its inner glow and emotional pull, is tolerant of what would otherwise be unsuccessful, but even so it is important to confine our study of the Amish use of color to the finest examples, and not to take an attitude of anything-goes because all Amish quilts are "in" at the moment. Wild and wonderful color schemes are sometimes successful in these quilts, but the most artistic Amish framed medallions rarely use more than two or three colors (often only one color and black). They do

42

however, frequently make successful use of several shades of the dominant color.

Even though the modern eye is tolerant and Amish custom beckons, then, we who walk into their tradition had best walk gingerly. We rarely find poor design among the Amish, because they accept the discipline of starkly simple inherited forms, and rarely elaborate them beyond the point of good taste. The same is not always true of their use of color, and if we want to be successful in our adaptations of classic forms, we should probably also accept a more or less rigid adherence to the classic laws of good color control.

Plates IX and X are Amish Bishop's Show quilts, illustrating the Bars and the Diamond in the Square patterns. The Bishop, who is the undisputed authority over all matters pertaining to the Amish community with which he is charged, is chosen by lot for life. The Bishop's quilts, presented to him at the time of his ordination, are made for him by the finest quiltmakers in the community, so that he will have prized possessions to show on the beds of his home when it is his turn to hold the Sunday services, which are always held in individual homes.

Both Plates IX and X illustrate, as all Amish framed medallions do, the special appropriateness of the Amish framed medallion for showing off the fine quilting for which these women are famous. Both these quilts have a feather scroll in the outside border, designed to loop into the corner, and, after a few flourishes, to terminate at the midpoints. This border, if you wish to adapt it, can be marked in the same way as those we did in Chapter II by first drawing in the stem outlines, and then filling in the feather segments by tracing around a template.

The corner squares in this kind of a quilt are usually ignored as separate design elements (as in Plates IX and X) but this is not always the case. A meandering feather is often interrupted by the use of a feather wreath in the corner squares, and other motifs - such as baskets - are sometimes used in the corner squares.

The inner borders rarely have continuous quilting designs. The corners of the inner borders often (as in these two photographs) have a small floral or feather wreath design quite unconnected with the design used in the rest of the inner border, which is frequently the popular pumpkin-seed border used in Plate X.

The use of all-over square diamonds in the entire center of a Bars quilt, as in Plate IX, is common, although we occasionally see cables, feathers, or other border patterns running along the individual bars. A feather wreath, or a star surrounded by a feather as in Plate X, is a common quilting design for a central square, and use of the small square diamonds in the triangles surrounding the central medallion is almost universal among museum-quality Diamond in the Square quilts.

The Square Diamond, which is easy to mark and quick to execute, is much used in all Amish framed medallions, even in large central areas such as the centers of the simple quilts shown in Figures 12-a and 12-b. While this type of

PLATE IX
Bars Quilt. Amish Bishop's Show Quilt, Lancaster County, Pennsylvania, c. 1915. This 80" x 80" all-wool quilt has a red outside border with electric blue corner blocks. The bars are mauve and blue, and the double small border is set off by four small peacock blue blocks. Note the quilting, which counts out at fifteen stitches per inch.

Collection of Barbara S. Janos and Barbara Ross, New York City

44

PLATE X
Diamond in the Square, Amish Bishop's Show Quilt, Lancaster County, Pennsylvania, c. 1918. All wool. The central medallion and the wide outside border are red; the large corner squares and the triangles which square out the central medallion are black; the narrow borders are peacock blue with emerald corners. The quilt is lined with orange silk. Note especially the superb quilting.

Collection of Barbara S. Janos and Barbara Ross, New York City

quilt might seem to present the perfect opportunity for fancier quilting, it must be remembered that these were utility quilts which were in great demand for ordinary use and which had to be made quickly in considerable numbers. The Amish mother not only had to supply her own large family with quilts, but was expected to supply an even dozen for each of her children when they set up housekeeping. It is also a fact that the close-set square diamond provides the perfect contrast to a fancy feather or cable border, and is possibly the best choice in any case. Good quilting design, in Amish as in other quilts, demands both contrast and restraint, and the effect of the simple framed medallion format is destroyed if it becomes, sampler-like, merely a vehicle for displaying the virtuosity of the quilter. So, in your planning of the quilting, at least until you are experienced enough to know instinctively what is effective, err on the side of too little rather than too much. Never stop studying quilt design on the quilts you get a chance to look at, and look especially among the Amish and the Welsh for fine examples of quilting, both in terms of design and of execution.

The Cable

The cable is much used on Amish borders, as it is on English framed medallions, and is not difficult to make once you get the general hang of it.

At first glance, we would assume that the cable had its origin as a two-dimensional representation of a rope, and indeed early American quilters did call it a rope. This design, however, has been in continuous use in the Mediterranean countries since the dawn of history. It is believed by art experts to be a magic Sumerian water symbol. Succeeding civilizations also used it as a magic or religious symbol, and we even see it on Greek vases and in Roman tiles. We know the cable continued to be used as a water symbol even into medieval times because bands of this water cable pattern running crosswise from a common center in the inlaid marble pavements of medieval Christian churches are traditionally held to represent the four rivers of paradise.

Probably the cable design came to England with the returning crusaders, who saw it in the Mediterranean. We don't know, of course, when it became a quilting design, but by the time it comes into the province of quilt history, it had obviously been in use for a long time. It was called a twist in England and a rope in America. It was a favorite early American design and was much used by carpenters, cabinetmakers, and silversmiths, as well as by quiltmakers. After 1858, when the first Atlantic telegraph cable was laid, however, the design was always called a cable (sometimes, even, an Atlantic Cable) on this side of the Atlantic, although it continued to be the twist in England, and still is.

The dream of the nineteenth century for fast communication between England and America seemed just as fanciful and impossible of achievement as the twentieth-century dream of putting a man on the moon. And when the first Atlantic telegraph cable was successfully laid in August of 1858 between Newfoundland and Ireland after many dangers, disasters, and false starts, the news created a sensation. The **Times** flatly stated that the Atlantic had dried up, and England and America had become one country again. Psalm 19, verse 4, "Their line is gone out through all the earth, and their words to the end of the world" was taken as the text of countless sermons. When Queen Victoria's 99-word message to President Buchanan, which took 16½ hours to transmit, finally got through, parades were organized and wild celebrations broke out all over the United States, including one in New York City in which the roof of the City Hall was ignited by fireworks, to the great detriment of the entire structure.

Soon afterward, the first commercial message was sent: "Mr. Cunard wishes telegraph McIver Europe collision Arabia. Put into St. John's. No lives lost." Before the end of the month Newfoundland signalled "Pray give some news for New York, they are mad for news", and the first press dispatch came across in response. New York discovered then that the Emperor of France had returned to Paris; the King of Prussia was too ill to visit Queen Victoria; the Chinese empire had been opened to trade; and the Gwalior insurgent army would be broken up and all India was becoming tranquil.

The fact that the cable broke soon afterward and was not replaced for a number of years did not dim the American quilter's enthusiasm for it, and the rope design continued to be called the Cable, as it is to this day.

How to Mark a Cable Border

Marking a cable border on a quilt is a simple matter. To mark a practice cable, trace the template given in Figure 15 on to cardboard, and cut it out. Rule a vertical line along the edge of a piece of scratchpaper.

Place the template so that the top left curve touches the ruled line, as in Figure 15. This ruled line represents the seam line, or a line of quilting along the edge of the border. If, in actual use, no such line exists, chalk one in as a guideline.

Mark along both sides of the template, as in Figure 15. Then move the template upward, so that the upper curve is still against the line of the border and so that the lower outside curve combines in such a way with the previously drawn "S" that the "eye" of the cable is the size you want it to be. Continue on in the same way, making sure that your outside curve touches the line of the border, and that the eyes are uniform in size and in shape.*

When you have mastered the technique, experiment with different sizes and shapes of cables. The appearance of the cable can be altered not only by changing the size and shape of the template (you can design your template with curves varying all the way from Marilyn Monroe to Twiggy), but by the angle at which it is held and by the size and shape of the "eye" which you create. No two women, even using the same template, will create quite the same cable, and this is one of the advantages of marking your own quilting instead of using a commercial pattern.

*In actual practice, when you are marking an entire border and know the angle of the template needed to produce the cable you want, it is easier to work with both borders marked, instead of one. Make a practice cable just as you want your border to be and measure its width. Then, mark two parallel guidelines. You'll find the marking goes faster, and that it is easier to keep the "eye" the same size when you are working between two lines than it is when you are working along one only.

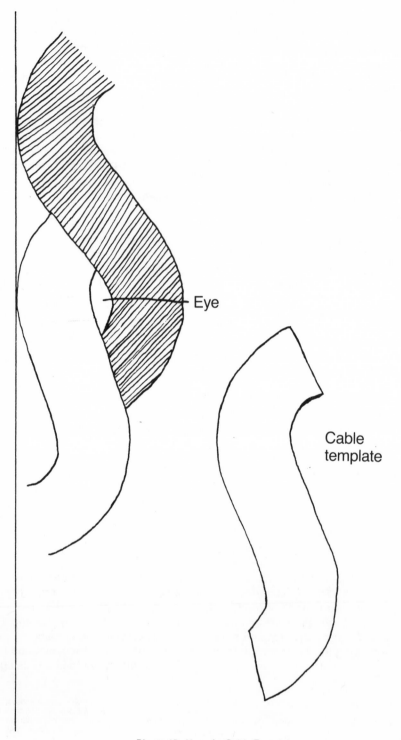

Eye

Cable
template

Figure 15 - Use of a Cable Template

48

Cable Corners

There is an old superstition to the effect that a broken cable on a quilt fore-tells a similar abrupt break in the life or fortunes of the quiltmaker, and most American quiltmakers went to great lengths, when quilting with a cable, to get around the corners somehow. The Amish, however, were apparently untouched by this superstition (as they were by the one which decreed that hearts could be put only on marriage or crib quilts lest the maker suffer some form of single blessedness) and we find their cables either interrupted by florals or feather wreaths at the corners (a perfectly acceptable resolution for the non-super-stitious) or even wandering off the edges of the quilts as if they were strippies, much to the detriment of the design.

It is perfectly possible to get around a corner with a cable, and there is no excuse for simply running off the side of the quilt. With most borders, we start in the corner and work out, making any necessary adjustments at the midpoints. A cable border, however, is easier to adjust in the corners, where things are a little strange anyway. Start at the bottom and work toward the upper lefthand corner. As you get into the corner, leave about a half a template's worth of space, reverse your template and start marking away from the corner at right angles as in Figure 16a. Once this pattern has been established, go back and design the corner. A careful study of Figure 16a-b-c and the comments given there should give you all the preparation you need for a practice session.

Sometimes the lines of a corner like the one in Figure 16c are drawn like those in Figure 17, so that it looks as if the strand were still twisted. This particular illustration is drawn using a taller, less curved template (given to the right in Figure 17) and produces an entirely different effect. Although 16-c is far and away the most common cable corner in use, Figure 17 seems to me to fit the demands of the cable form better, and is certainly no harder to construct.

Adjusting the Shape of a Framed Medallion

The framed medallion is a beautiful format for a square quilt, and most framed medallions are square. However, unless you are designing a quilt to hang on the wall, or to use on a Queen-sized bed, the square shape is not functional. It is perfectly simple, however, to reshape the central medallion of the quilts in Figures 12 and 13 so that the quilt can take the shape of any bed. A diamond can be substituted for the central square in any of the quilts in Figure 14 to accomplish the same purpose.

Other Framed Medallions

The quilts in Figure 12 can be further varied, as they are among the Amish, by substituting patchwork for the central square, and adding borders of the same materials as used in the patchwork. These make effective quilts no matter what patchwork pattern is chosen, or how the squares are set together, particularly if the quilt is intended to be hung in a gallery or show. The Crib Quilt in Plate XII

Figure 16a - Construction of a Cable Corner, Step 1
   When you get into the corner, reverse your template, and, leaving a space about half a template wide, start working away from the corner. This is usually easier if you turn your work so that you can work down instead of left-to-right.

Figure 16b - Construction of a Cable Corner, Step 2
Fill in the lines across the space left in the corner.

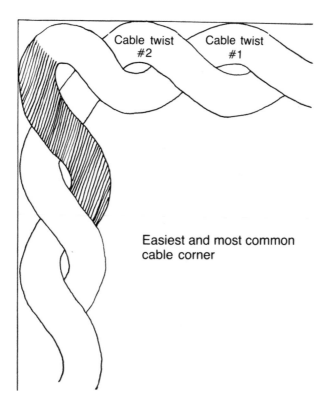

Cable twist
#2

Cable twist
#1

Easiest and most common
cable corner

Figure 16c - Construction of a Cable Corner, Step 3.
　　Take your template again and trace it in the position of the shaded template. Turn
the template over and place it so that the right-hand side of it joins up where Cable
Twist #1 would reappear were it to come out from behind Cable Twist 2. Some slight
adjustments will have to be made to make this fit smoothly at the top. It can be done
freehand, or by the simple means of not tracing the entire template.

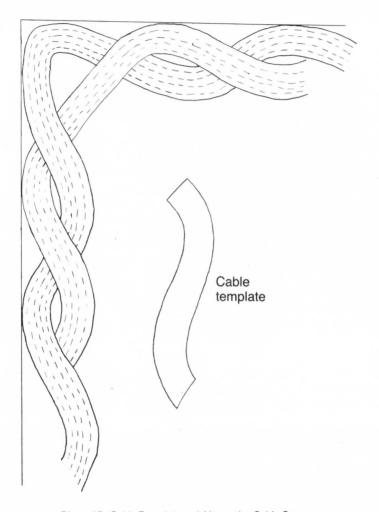

Figure 17 - Cable Template and Alternative Cable Corner.

and Love Ring, Plate XIX, both in Chapter IV, are good examples of this approach. Also, compare the crazy quilt from the Royal Ontario Museum, Plate XXXV, Chapter VII to Figure 12-b, for a further interpretation of the basic framed medallion.

It can be seen, then, that the framed medallion, which fell into disuse because it had abandoned itself to clutter, still has a lot of mileage in it, and is easily adapted to the tastes and needs of the modern quiltmaker. It is a high-style utility quilt, quickly made, perfectly adapted to wool, and will undoubtedly find more and more acceptance as we turn our thermostats lower and lower and find ourselves faced with the same pressing demand for warm bedcoverings that kept our great-grandmothers busy with their needles.

PATCHWORK QUILTS

Nowhere has the current quilt revival showed its contemporary force more clearly than in the patchwork quilt. Exciting experiments are being carried out with color, in which extremely artistic shadings from dark to light move across the quilt - sometimes diagonally - sometimes as if a spotlight were on the center of the quilt, leaving the edges in darkness. Other artists are working with "bending" the shapes of the blocks. That is not to say that there are not historical examples of either, for there are, but there is little prior exploration in these areas of quiltmaking. They are a sophisticated contemporary expression and will undoubtedly lead us on to even greater visual excitement.

We have been fortunate, in this quilt revival, to have artists choosing textiles rather than pigments as a medium of expression. But these patchwork artists are not working in an artistic vacuum. Most, if not all, base their work solidly on the traditional patterns and traditional methods which found their first American expression almost at the beginning of our colonial history.

Fabric was scarce in the colonies, and every scrap was pressed into service. While no wool utility quilts of the type that later, out in the midwest, came to be known as "hired man's" quilts, have survived, it doesn't take much imagination to picture them in our minds. Many - particularly those the children (of both sexes) worked on - were undoubtedly put together from simple squares - random patches, four patches, nine-patches. Probably because these people came from an enriched artistic background, they were set with due concern for color interest and held together by a border of some kind. In the hands of other members of the extended family, particularly as the first pressures of establishing themselves in the wilderness eased, squares were undoubtedly, then as now, used in eye-catching patterns like the Irish Chains, Around the World, or Burgoyne's Surrender, all of which are perfectly adapted to wool.

Some of these quilts were undoubtedly made from discarded clothing, but scraps left over from construction of new clothing would have been available as well. In New England and Canada, these quilts would have been lined with heavy, partly worn-out blankets or clothing, or with many layers of batting, and therefore could not be quilted easily and quickly because of their excessive thickness. They were tied instead.

Eventually, quiltmakers got used to seeing the patterns that are best adapted to wool tied rather than quilted and these favorite patterns have been handed down to us as tied quilts. Crazy quilts, Chapter VII, the lovely Rocky Road to Kansas*, and many of the pressed quilts in Chapter VI are in this category.

*See **Galaxy of Stars: America's Favorite Quilts** by Jean Dubois p. 66-70 for pattern, directions, and photos of this quilt, as well as for a discussion of its origins.

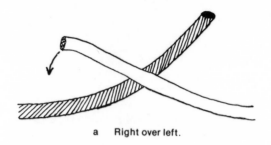

a   Right over left.

b   Grab the cord that has been in your right hand with your left, pull it under and
over.

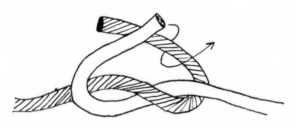

c   Left over right.

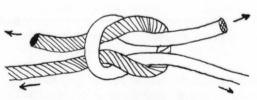

d   The finished square knot, just before being tightened. You will note that all the
tying was done with the cord that was originally in your right hand.

Figure 18 - How to Tie a Square Knot

In addition to factors of time and weight, there are also artistic considerations involved in the decision of whether to tie or to quilt. There are times when tying contributes to the design statement being made better than quilting could. Certainly there is a long tradition of tying wool quilts, and we should consider this possibility whenever we have a wool quilt to finish. If the decision is to tie, it should not be approached as a simple problem in logistics, however. There is more to tying than putting a tie every two inches to keep the batting in place. Ties need to be fairly close together, but they can be placed in such a way as to re-enforce the design. The cotton and linen nine-patch in Plate XI is a good example of a quilt whose design was strengthened by the placement of the ties.

Wool batts are the warmest, of course, and have always been used in England, even in cotton comforters. They are beginning to be popular on this side of the Atlantic as well (see Chapter III). Neither a wool nor a cotton batt can be put in the washing machine unless it is closely quilted to hold it in place, however, so worn blankets or dacron battings are sometimes used instead. A comforter that really comforts usually has several battings between its layers.

How to Tie a Quilt

A comforter that is not going to see hard wear can be tied with lengths of yarn. Donna Renshaw uses a length of yarn about two yards long, pulled double in a sharp darning needle, and works across the comforter in a systematic way, taking one-fourth-inch stitches through all three layers at each point where a tie is to be made. She does not cut the yarn in between stitches until she is ready to tie. Just as in quilting, she advises the craftswoman to keep her left hand under the work, to make sure the needle comes all the way through and catches the bottom layer in the stitch. When all the stitches have been taken, she cuts the threads midway between the stitches, and ties square knots as tightly as possible.

Tying is a nice group or family project, and when it comes to making square knots (and square knots **are** essential if your work is to stay together), your Brownie or Cub Scout has a real chance to shine. One personal demonstration of square-knot tying by a seven-year-old kid is a lot more use than a diagram, but those of you who have to go it alone should start by consulting Figure 18.

As you can see, you tie the entire knot by working with the rope end that was originally in your right hand. The square knot is best practiced with a length of venetian blind cord, so that you can see what you are doing and so that you can test whether the final knot **is** a square knot or simply the lowly granny. The finished knot should look like Diagram d, Figure 18. A true square knot tied in venetian blind cord is easily untied by pushing toward the center with both ends of the cord.

As any former Brownie can tell you, it's easy to tie a square knot with a diagram in front of you. The crunch comes when you're out in the woods with rope and no diagram. So the Brownies have devised this magic incantation, which they whisper to themselves every time they make a square knot, and which

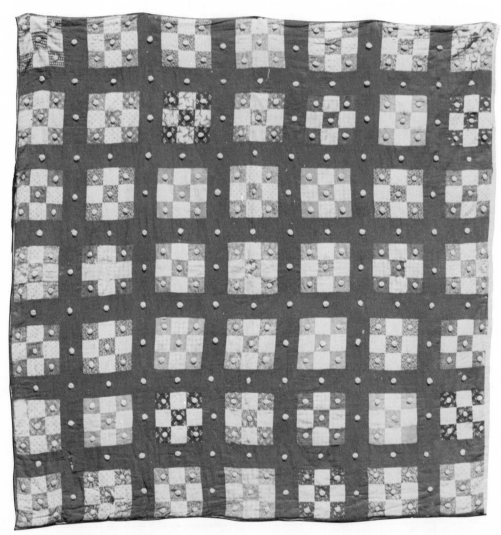

PLATE XI
Cotton Nine-patch, with red linen latticework, Colorado c. 1876, made from a variety of quiet prints artistically arranged so that the blue blocks radiate out from the center. Note the surface interest generated by the size and placing of the wool pompons. Backing is a small blue and white print.

will work for you too:

Right over left
And left over right
Makes a knot
That's tidy and tight.

An older method of quilt tying than Donna's, and one which, if the surviving examples prove a point, can take more wear and tear, involves the use of heavy button and carpet thread for the knot, which is tied (again with a square knot) around lengths of yarn or unspun wool, as in pompon-making. This is well described by Thelma Newman, who advocates the use, in quilt tying, of a curved upholstery needle. She starts from the top, catches the battings and lining in a one-fourth-inch stitch, and then returns to the top and cuts her thread so that she has about two inches of it on each side of the stitch. She then places a 1½" length of yarn at right angles to the two ends of carpet thread and knots the carpet thread twice or three times, and then knots the yarn, twice. She later trims all the tufts to the same length. The difference between tufts and pompons is that pompons have several strands of yarn or a tuft of wool at right angles to the thread rather than a single strand, as Thelma uses.

Your choice of method and material for the tying should be influenced by the quilt's materials, design, and function. The large wool pompons on the cotton and linen quilt pictured in Plate XI add contrast, three-dimensionality, and interest to a simple nine-patch. The tiny ribbon-bows in Plate XX add interest and excitement to this wool Grandmother's Fan, and they are still in perfect condition after almost eighty years of use.

A square knot, of course, is not the only knot, and you might want to think about the effectiveness of the French knots used to tie down the pressed octagons in the Evening Star quilt pictured in Plate XVIII.

TRIANGLES - ALONE OR IN COMPANY

The use of wool in patchwork is by no means limited to simple squares. Anything that can be done in cotton can be done in wool, if you are careful not to stretch the patches along the bias. Beginners should stick to simple shapes and good-sized pieces however, and the many quilts which are made with simple triangles are perfect for a beginner, as well as for an experienced quiltmaker whose main interest is in getting a top together in a hurry.

Birds in Flight

Birds in Flight, an early 19th-century strippie pattern, is one of the easiest of these, and if worked with large triangles, can be worked up quickly and easily on the machine. Its basic pattern pieces are an equilateral triangle and two right triangles sewed together to make a rectangle. These rectangles are then sewed together into strips of whatever length the quilt needs to be, and interspersed with unpatched strips.

Make your pattern by cutting a rectangle that's twice as long as it is wide. 3½" x 7" is a good size for a double bed. Measure **exactly**. If your pattern is a little off, your quilt will be a disaster.

Fold the rectangle in half, forming two squares, and crease along this center line, which represents our midpoint. Unfold. Now, bring the lower left-hand corner up to the midpoint at the top of the rectangle. What used to be the bottom of the left-hand side of the rectangle now lies exactly along the midpoint fold, and what used to be the left-hand side of the rectangle now lies along the top. Crease.

Now, bring the lower right-hand corner up to the midpoint and crease. If all went well, you should have an equilateral triangle topped with two right triangles. Cut out and label the large triangle "A" and one of the small triangles "B". Make your templates by mounting these triangles on cardboard or buckram, adding your ¼" seam allowance, measuring exactly.*

On cotton quilts, I think the easiest way to get accurate pattern pieces is to draw around these templates with a sharp pencil. With wool, which slips, slithers, and slides, however, it is hard to trace an accurate pattern. It is better, I think, to cut out paper patterns, pin them firmly on the wool, and cut around them. Never use a paper pattern too long however, as tiny slivers inadvertently cut off the edges of the paper pattern as the cutting progresses eventually change its shape enough to throw off the accuracy of the entire block. If you find this unbelievable, cut 30 triangles from the same paper pattern, and then compare #1 with #30. Remember that a tiny inaccuracy many times repeated has drastic consequences in patchwork. It is not a medium for a sloppy craftswoman.

Cut out two B's for every A, and keep in mind when cutting that the A's are the birds flying and should be cut out of the dominant colors, while the B's are the background.

It would be a shame to tie a strippie quilt, which presents such marvelous opportunities for quilting. The triangles could be outlined (by quilting ¼" in from the seam lines), to re-enforce the strong geometry of the quilt, and for contrast the unpatched strips could be quickly and easily done in a Durham Feather (Chapter II) or a Cable (Chapter III).

There is an interesting modern setting, "The Forest for the Trees", diagrammed in the Gutcheons' book, which you might want to look at if you're planning a Birds in Flight-type quilt.**

If you are seriously interested in working on the modern fringe of patchwork, I would recommend a thorough study of **The Quilt Design Workbook**. Although they have not departed from the traditional block, the Gutcheons, both in their settings and in their use of color, have lifted patchwork far above the humdrum level on which it is so often practiced.

*Check the pattern pieces given for the Basket Quilt, Figure 19, to see how to handle the seam allowance on triangles.

Gutcheon, Beth and Jeffrey, **The Quilt Design Workbook, p. 103.

PLATE XII
Triangle Variation Crib Quilt, Amish, Ohio, c. 1918. This quilt has a bold, graphic color combination in which the usual nursery pinks and blues are allowed to explode into pink, mauve, and maroon; bright blue and navy.

Collection of Barbara S. Janos and Barbara Ross, New York City

The Triangle Variation Crib Quilt

Another quilt which uses simple strips of triangles with glamorous effect is the Triangle Variation Crib Quilt in Plate XII.* Although, because the black and white film could not entirely capture the subtleties of color in this quilt, the five dark strips look plain, the central medallion of this bordered quilt is constructed entirely of right triangles sewed into strips. However, a quilt **could** be planned with strips of plain wool alternating with double strips of patched triangles for a bolder, simpler version of this strong diagonal pattern.

To reproduce this quilt, draft your triangle pattern by folding a square in half diagonally. Start in the lower left corner with one triangle. Add, successively, strips of 3, 5, 7, 9, 11, and 13 triangles. You have now reached the center of the top, where you will need to add two rows containing 14 triangles each. Now, continuing on toward the upper right-hand corner, add, successively, rows containing 13, 11, 9, 7, 5, 3, and 1 triangle. Border, first with a narrow, and then with a wider band of wool, picking up the two colors used in the triangles that you wish to dominate the whole, and mitring the corners for a more professional look.

Another dazzling quilt that can be made with this same triangle pattern is Molly Upton's **Fanfare**, pictured on p. 123 of **The Quilt Design Workbook**.

Baskets

Baskets, many of which had a New England origin, were great favorites with 19th and early 20th-century American quiltmakers. They look difficult, but are usually accomplished with only three pattern pieces - a square and two triangles. Use the pattern pieces in Figure 19 to make a basket like the one on the quilt in Plate XIII. Before you cut pieces for an entire top with this pattern, as for any other in this book, always make a sample block. Kathy, who is a real expert in the field, drafted all the patterns, and I have tried them out and found them true. Nevertheless, the printed page goes through many processes before it reaches you, and small distortions may creep in. The materials you use, or small differences in your personal patching technique, may affect results as well. During the course of making a sample block, moreover, you may discover that the technique required to make the pattern is not compatible with your temperament or your special abilities, and you will thus save yourself months of frustration by eliminating that particular pattern from consideration.

Sample blocks so made need not be wasted. Some homemakers frame them and hang them on the wall. Some make beautiful pillows. Other smart ladies make all their samples in the same colors and materials and eventually combine them into sampler quilts.

To make a sample block, you will need:

1 red #1 triangle	9 red #2 triangles	7 black #3 squares
1 black #1 triangle	9 black #2 triangles	

*When equilateral triangles (half-diamonds) are put together in strips like this, the pattern is usually called Streak of Lightning, or the more prosaic Zigzag. These triangles are right triangles (squares cut in half diagonally) and give a softer line, more suitable for a crib quilt.

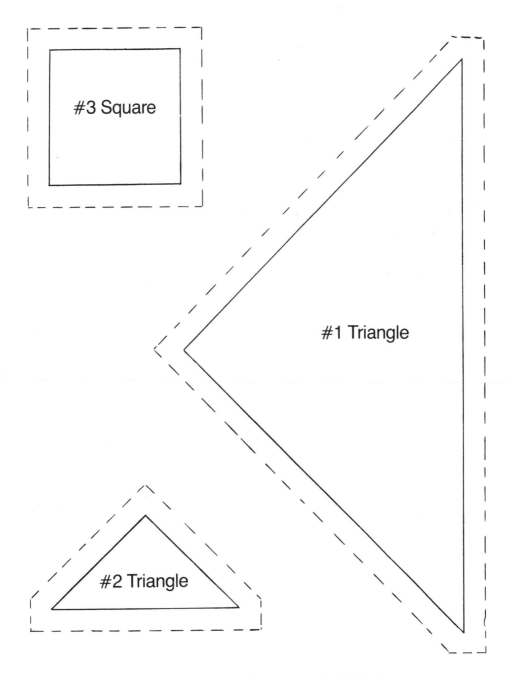

Figure 19 - Pattern Pieces for the Basket Quilt, 6" block

This block, because it is small (6" square), is more difficult than some of the other blocks in this book, and is not recommended as your first adventure in working with wool. It makes an extremely effective wool quilt, however, and once you are accustomed to working with wool, shouldn't give you any trouble.

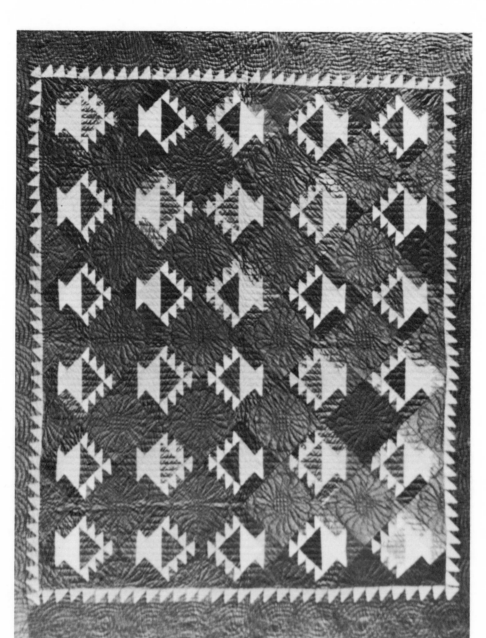

To assemble:

1. Combine the two #1 triangles into a square. Combine all the #2 red triangles with the black triangles into squares. Press the seams open.

2. Lay three of these squares out in a row with the black part of the squares to the upper left and the red part to the lower right. Holding them in this position, sew them into a strip. Press. In general, I press seams open, for a smoother look on the front side, and so that I never have to quilt through two thicknesses, but in this pattern there are a number of joinings where a smoother effect can be had from pressing the seam to one side. They will become immediately apparent to you as you work.

3. Holding the large square made in Step 1 so that the red is on the lower right and the black is on the upper left, add the strip made in Step 2 across the top. Note that the red triangles in both assemblies are on the lower right. Sew and press.

4. Lay out, from left to right, 2 black #3 squares, and a red-and-black square with the red to the upper left. Sew into a strip and press. Add to the assembly made in Step 3, along the bottom of the large square.

5. Lay out a strip as follows: #3 black square; 4 combination squares, with the red on the lower left. Sew, press, and add to the left-hand side of the large assembly, with the black square to the bottom. Press.

6. Working from left to right, lay out a strip as follows: #2 black; #2 black; #2 black; combination square with red on lower left; #2 black. Sew, press, and add to the right-hand side of the large assembly with the three black squares to the top.

You should now have a completed basket block. Compare with Plate XIII to make sure you have all the components in the right places.

These directions sound much more confusing than they are, and once you have made one block, many suggestions for speeding up the work will present themselves to your mind.

The Amish Basket in Plate XIII is interesting because of its use of red wool in combination with black sateen, not only because of the exciting difference in texture, but because the light is reflected back from the sateen with greater intensity than from the wool. This makes for a more interesting surface than could have been achieved by the use of either one material or the other. You will note, particularly among the blacks, that this is a scrap quilt and thus has an integrity that no quilt made from especially-bought lengths of material can have.

The setting of this quilt is unusual, because the basket block is usually set diagonally, either with alternate unpatched blocks in print or a contrasting color, or with lattice strips, and is usually not bordered, except among the Amish.

Baskets are usually quilted ¼" inside the seam lines of the triangles to re-enforce the angular lines of the basket, and I prefer that design to the all-over parallel lines used in the Amish quilt in Plate XIII. The alternate block frequently exhibits a curved pattern, often a feather wreath, as in Plate XIII. See Chapter II for directions for marking a feather wreath. The quilted cable which is used in the border of this quilt is demonstrated in Chapter III.

For a dazzling modern setting, in which the individual baskets are lost in a blaze of geometry, see Plate 15 in Jonathan Holstein's **The Pieced Quilt: An American Design Tradition**. At first, you'll be hard put to convince yourself that this quilt, which is one of the real design triumphs of 20th-century quiltmaking, **is** a basket quilt. A little study, however, will show that the lattice framework, about half the width of the blocks, is arranged in a simple tic-tac-toe. Four basket blocks, set together with their handles in the outer corners, are put into the central square. Two baskets, set side-by-side with the handles outward, go above; two below; and two to each side of the central square; and a basket with its handle reaching inward is set in each corner.

Stars

Simple star patterns such as the Ohio Star and the Sawtooth Star (pictured in the Frontispiece), are ideally adapted to wool or to combinations, such as wool and cotton. Since I gave the patterns for both of these simple stars in **Galaxy***, I will not repeat them here. They are usually set with alternate blocks, or with lattice strips, but they also make breath-taking all-over quilts. (See Figure 20)

Another interesting set for an Ohio Star, which I copied from an early 19th-century Wyoming quilt, has triangles in each corner of the setting blocks which, when combined with the pieced star blocks, forms neckties. Quickly machine-made, I gave it a thoroughly modern look by making it up in red cotton flannel and printed wool challis. As in the Amish Basket (Plate XIII), the cotton reflects back the light more boldly than the wool does, providing a unique and vibrant surface.

Twentieth-century quiltmakers have realized that every block in a quilt doesn't have to be the same size. Anne Orr, in the early part of the century, owed much of her design success with applique to this realization, and contemporary patchworkers have based many interesting designs on this concept. Beth Gutcheon's "The Star Also Rises", an all-over design, surrounds a large central star block with a ring of smaller star blocks, and then squares out the quilt with yet smaller star blocks.** There are other, more sophisticated ways of altering block sizes, however.

Some 20th-century innovators have had breath-taking results with altering the size of the block components as they work out from the middle of the quilt toward the edges, sometimes increasing the size of the block as they work outward, sometimes decreasing it. This is not an entirely new idea, as it was

---

*Dubois, Jean, **A Galaxy of Stars: America's Favorite Quilts**. Sawtooth Star, p. 27-9; Ohio Star p. 3-8. See also Tippecanoe and Tyler Too, p. 14 & 15.

Gutcheon, Beth and Jeffrey, **The Quilt Design Workbook, Plate X, and pp. 72-3.

Figure 20 - Ohio Star, set solid.

widely used in the design of the 18th-century framed medallions, but it is a revolutionary idea when applied to the block-type quilt, and has produced some truly 20th-century opticals unlike anything in the tradition which created them. Bonnie and Mary Leman, working with the Yankee Puzzle*, which, although made entirely of triangles, is a close relative of the Ohio Star, created a spectacular quilt using this technique. A close examination of Figure 21b shows that, by their use of color choices, the Lemans made the Yankee Puzzle show forth the basic Ohio Star in ever-widening circles around a central one.** Because of gradations in triangle size, the central yellow-and-green circle seems to be surrounded by a circle of stars (four pink and blue; four green and blue) and the circle is squared color-wise by four more yellow-and-blue stars in the corners, although the circling continues, structurally.

This kind of quilt, while it keeps the old block pattern, has to be constructed in rows rather than blocks because the size of the components keeps changing. Each block as you work outward from the center is ½" smaller than the one before it, so you have to keep drafting new patterns as you work.

Start with the central square in Figure 21. It is 9½" square. To get your pattern for the triangle in this square, draft a 9½" square and fold it diagonally, twice. Cut two yellow triangles and two from the background color. (**Quilter's Newsletter Magazine** used a grayish blue). The squares above, below, and to the left and right of the central block are 9½" x 9", so you will need to draft a new pattern, based on a 9" x 9½" square.

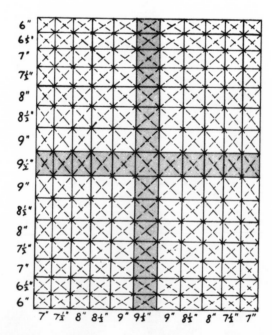

Figure 21a - Piecing Diagram for Contemporary Yankee Puzzle

***Quilter's Newsletter Magazine**, July 1976, p. 8-9.

**Reproduced in black and white in the present edition.

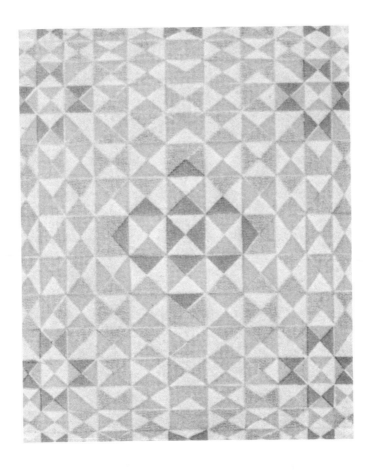

Figure 21b - Contemporary Yankee Puzzle designed by Bonnie and Mary Leman

You can see that the construction of one of these modern optical quilts is complicated, but the results are dazzling and may provide a vehicle for the idea you are trying to express. It would be a good idea, I think, to trace out a diagram like Figure 21 (only on a larger scale) and experiment with color schemes before embarking on a quilt of this type. Your final colored diagram would then provide an easy key for cutting and construction.

HEXAGONS

At one time, a friendship quilt was a common going-away present for a neighbor whose husband was pulling up stakes and moving farther west, both because her family need the warmth the quilt could provide out on the raw new frontier, and because she needed the moral support of knowing she had friends who cared enough about her to send a part of themselves along into her new life. Even today, I don't know of any group project that is more satisfying to everyone involved than undertaking a friendship quilt, nor can I imagine any greater thrill than receiving one.

Ava's Friendship Quilt

The Album Patch and the Odd Fellow's Cross are common friendship quilts*, but the slightly more sophisticated pattern diagrammed in Figure 22, which comes from the collection of Ava Humble of Durango, Colorado, is unique, interesting to piece, and beautifully adapted to wool. It is also well adapted to machine piecing, so even the busiest members of a club or quilt guild can participate. The pattern pieces for an 18" block are given in Figure 23a & b.

Figure 22 - Diagram for Ava's Friendship Quilt

*The crazy quilt, discussed in Chapter VII, was also frequently used as a friendship quilt.

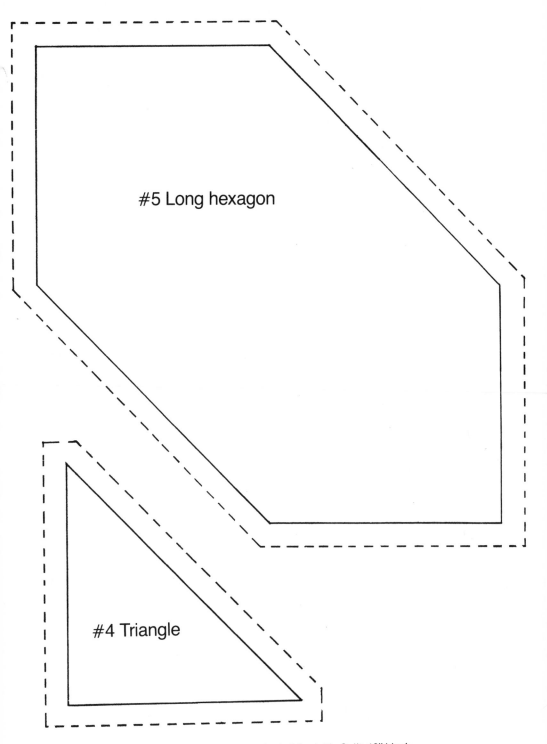

#5 Long hexagon

#4 Triangle

Figure 23a - Pattern pieces, Ava's Friendship Quilt, 18" block.

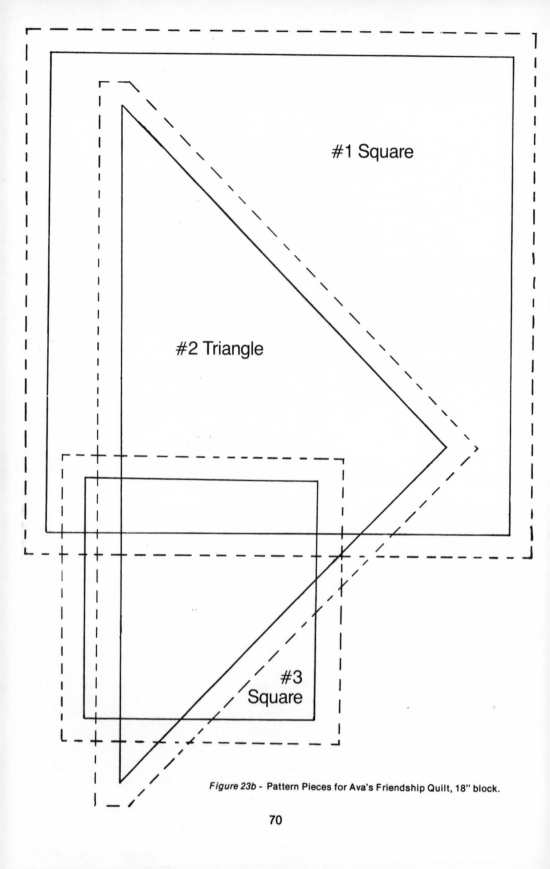

#1 Square

#2 Triangle

#3
Square

Figure 23b - Pattern Pieces for Ava's Friendship Quilt, 18" block.

Once a suitable number of these blocks has been assembled, they can be set with lattice strips or alternate plain blocks. A group, however, might prefer to buy a length of wool for the #2 corner triangles, the #3 squares and the #4 triangles which frame the central hexagon, so that the blocks can be set together as an all-over quilt, leaving the individuals to harmonize their color choices in the hexagon, the #1 squares, and the remaining triangles. It would thus be possible to achieve good color control without giving up individuality.

Some thought should also be given, in the planning stage, to providing space for dedicating, dating, and signing the quilt, so that it will be truly commemorative.

To piece, first combine the #5 hexagon with two #4 triangles. Make the corner blocks by combining the #3 square and two #4 triangles, and then with a #2 triangle, pressing as you go.

After checking with the diagram in Figure 22 to make sure that none of your corner pieces gets in upside down, assemble the block in three strips as follows:

1. a corner block; a #4 square; a corner block
2. a #4 square; the central hexagon block; a #4 square
3. a corner block; a #4 square; a corner block.

After pressing the seams in the three strips, sew them together into a square. Be certain, when assembling, that the #3 squares are all placed toward the center of the block.

Finally, embroider your name, the date, or any comments you might want to make on the #5 hexagon in a contrasting color so it will show up well.

TRAPEZOIDS

The Windmill Cross

The Windmill Cross* (Plate XIV), because of its few pattern pieces and simple construction, is well adapted to wool, and can be designed either as an all-over quilt as in the photograph, or set with lattice strips or alternating plain squares.

This quilt, which my mother pieced in 1920, is an example of the scrap quilt at its finest, both in its superb handling of color and in its utilization of every scrap of available fabric. Many different materials were recycled into the dark trapezoids which form the crosses. One single block, for instance has navy-blue pieces from **five** different garments. All the trapezoids in each block were done either in black or in navy, and all the triangles in each block were done in one color, even where that required patching to form a large enough piece to cut the

*A similar quilt called the Colorado Quilt (Kansas City Star January 8, 1941) achieves the same result by breaking the trapezoids down into #1 triangles. I can't see any particular reason to do that much extra work unless your wools are all small scraps. The pattern for the Windmill Cross came from Mrs. S. R. Sherwin of Harvard, Nebraska.

PLATE XIV
Detail, Windmill Cross, wool and velvet, Lincoln, Nebraska, 1920. Pieced by Mrs. Forest R. Hall, now of Laramie, Wyoming.

triangle from.

Color control is entirely instinctive with mother, as it is with most good patchworkers. She uses miscellaneous colors - in this quilt navy, black, light blue, brown, tan, yellow, gold, purple, red, maroon, green, and gray - but she does not use them in a miscellaneous way. Three gold blocks, which tend to come forward to meet the eye are placed so they form a large visual triangle on the quilt top. While most designers shy away from the use of any material in only one block in a quilt, mother used single blocks of several colors without disastrous results. A single yellow block, which jumps out from the background, is balanced by an even more aggressive pale blue block and by a purple velvet one which attracts the eye because of the way the light strikes its different texture.

Mother used a soft red, of which she evidently had a great quantity, to tie the quilt together by placing the red blocks together in alternate horizontal stripes. This red fabric would certainly provide a means of dating the quilt if mother had not been able to authenticate the date, as it provides a typical example of the difficulties of U.S. fabric manufacturers when color-fast German dyes became unavailable during World War I. Although the fading may have improved the color - it is now a soft, romantic red - it has faded unevenly in places as if it were the result of a stovetop Rit-pot disaster.

Mom and I agree that she didn't do the world's best patching when she was a young thing, and that my maiden effort at quilting looks a bit as if a committee from the state hospital had done it, but that the quilt is breath-takingly beautiful even so. Maybe that's the real appeal of quiltmaking: there is always perfection to strive for; improvements to be enjoyed day by day; but the final result, however amateur, is entirely satisfactory.

The pattern given in Figure 24 produces a 12" block which can be set, as mother's quilt was, six across and seven down for a double-bed quilt. Each block requires:

16 #1 triangles, light
4 #2 trapezoids, dark
4 #3 trapezoids, dark

When you are planning your quilt, you might consider the fact that a fascinating all-over optical design results if the quilt is pieced in two colors only, with the trapezoids which make up the windmill in one color and the other pieces in another, strongly contrasted, color. When this is done, a feathered star develops on the diagonal while the windmill cross stands forth on the verticals and horizontals. When done in two colors only the pattern also develops grids of diagonally-set squares which tie the whole together as effectively as latticework would.

If you have beautiful Victorian furniture that you want to set off without its having to compete with crazy work, try this quilt in a monochrome of velveteen and wool for a rich, exciting Victorian texture which adds to the sumptuousness of the furniture without competing with it.

73

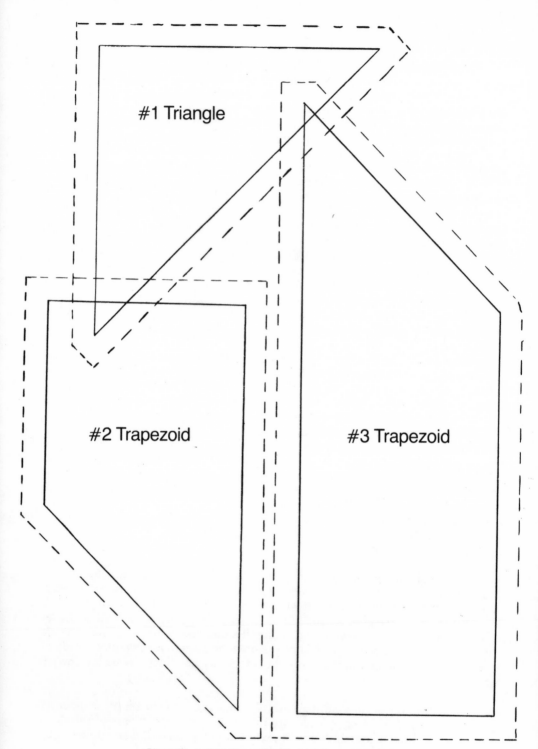

#1 Triangle

#2 Trapezoid

#3 Trapezoid

Figure 24 - pattern Pieces for Windmill Cross, 12" block.

74

The Pineapple

The pineapple quilt block is made up of a series of trapezoids, each one slightly larger than the one before it. It is sometimes constructed as a pieced quilt (and should be if you want to quilt it by hand) but because of the inherent stretchiness of the long wool strips involved, it is usually made by the pressed quilt method, and is therefore discussed in Chapter VI. Pattern pieces for the Pineapple Quilt are given in Figure 52a,b,c.

Nancy Crow

Nancy Crow (Plate XV) is a contemporary textile artist who is doing exciting things with simple shapes. Nancy, who lives and works in Athens, Ohio, does not use traditional blocks, but develops her own, similar ones. She begins by working out her ideas in a sketchbook, working freehand, rather than on graph paper, as she finds the lines and squares too inhibiting. She begins to use a ruler only when she is ready to draw the blocks to size and to draft the patterns.

Once the design is firm in her mind, Nancy works out "Information Sheets" which include sketches of the whole quilt, of one entire block, and of the repeat unit, as well as a listing of the number of pieces to be cut out. She then determines the size of the repeat block and drafts it full-size on heavy art paper. She then makes a duplicate of the unit, adds the seam allowances, and cuts out her patterns. She prefers this heavy paper to cardboard for patterns, as it is easier to cut, and a typical Nancy Crow quilt might have as many as forty different pattern pieces.

"I do not work the color combinations out on paper," Nancy says, "I find that much too inhibiting. So I usually make my designs in black and white. When it comes to choosing the colors, I choose intuitively. Before doing my sewing I pin the pieces up on my 8 ft. by 8 ft. wall made of Celotex (pressed paper board painted white on one side and soft enough for push pins). By pinning up my quilt pieces I can see how the colors work together and then make any needed changes. I never start sewing until I am sure - because I've done enough ripping to last a lifetime!"

When she is ready to cut, Nancy folds her fabric so that she can cut four layers at once. She keeps her scissors sharp, and always keeps three or four pairs on hand.

"When I am ready to start sewing," Nancy says, "I place my sewing machine at one end of an 8-foot-long table which is three feet wide. I lay out as many pattern pieces as possible on the table and begin joining them using no pins. I only use pins when I am joining the major parts of the blocks and when joining the blocks themselves. I also sew the pieces one after the other without cutting the thread between. I end up with a huge pile of pieces that must then be cut apart. However, this is a great way to save on thread and time."

Nancy doesn't do her own quilting, but she does mark her own tops before sending them off to be quilted by the Amish women near Charm, Ohio.

PLATE XV
Nancy Crow

Peter's Quilt

Peter's Quilt (Plate XVI), which Nancy designed in the fall of 1975, is a cotton quilt, but there is no reason it could not be done in wool as well. In fact, since it is intended to be made in plain colors only, wool would present a more vibrant, glowing surface.

This nine-block quilt is an all-over pattern, based on a 26" square (Figure 25) which is itself composed of four identical units. It can be seen, then, that this quilt is based on a simple repeat, which could be constructed like the pressed quilts in Chapter VI. When done in wool, the pressed technique would in fact be preferable, as it would prevent the long wool strips from stretching. Consider, however, the greater ease of quilting a pieced, as opposed to a pressed, quilt when making this decision.

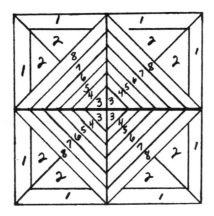

Figure 25 - Basic Block, Peter's Quilt.

A beautiful quilt, made with a simple color scheme, can be created using this pattern, but Nancy's quilt is an artistic triumph because of her sophisticated use of color. Peter's Quilt was made for Nancy's brother-in-law, Peter, who is a painter. "I had a stack of pastels on my work table," Nancy says, "and he waved his arm over them, saying he liked that bunch of colors."

Figure 26 shows Nancy's color key and the color code to read it by. To make the quilt in Nancy's original color scheme, you will need to cut the following pieces from the patterns given in Figure 27a & b.

#1	72 white	#2	16 beige	#3	8 turquoise
			16 very light salmon		4 golden orange
			16 off white		10 medium pink
			24 very light pink		2 very light pink
					12 salmon

(Cutting directions continued on page 83)

PLATE XVI
Peter's Quilt, designed and pieced by Nancy Crow, Athens, Ohio, 1975.

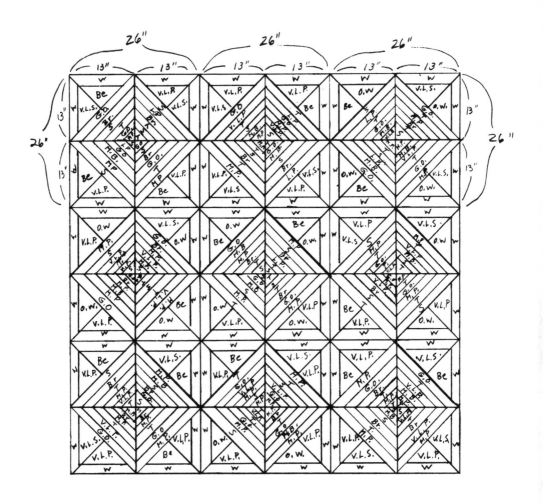

Figure 26 - Color Key and Color Code for Peter's Quilt.

Courtesy Nancy Crow

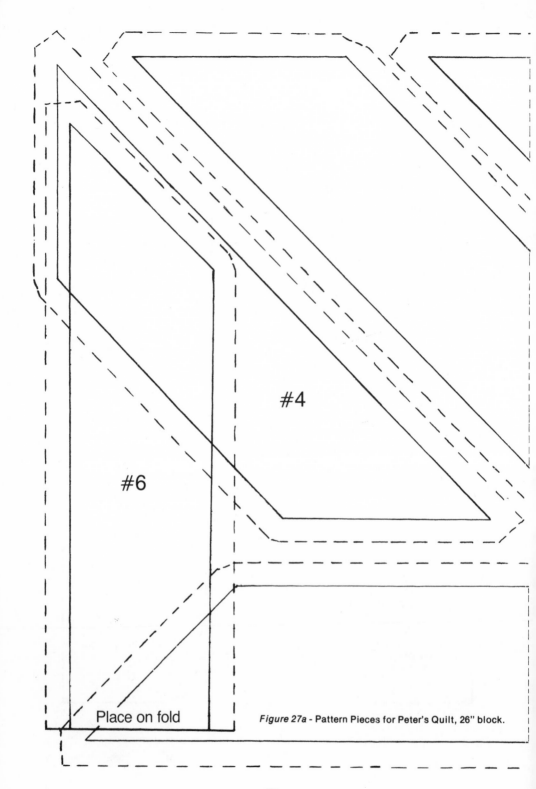

#4

#6

Place on fold

Figure 27a - Pattern Pieces for Peter's Quilt, 26" block.

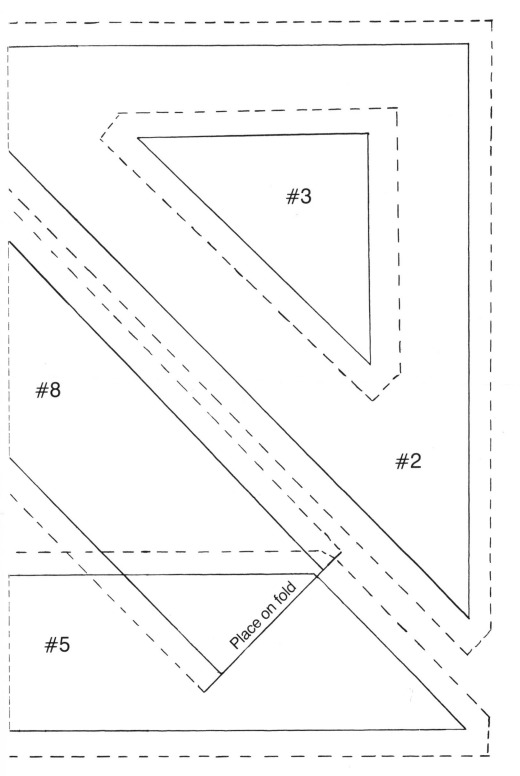

#3

#8

#2

#5

Place on fold

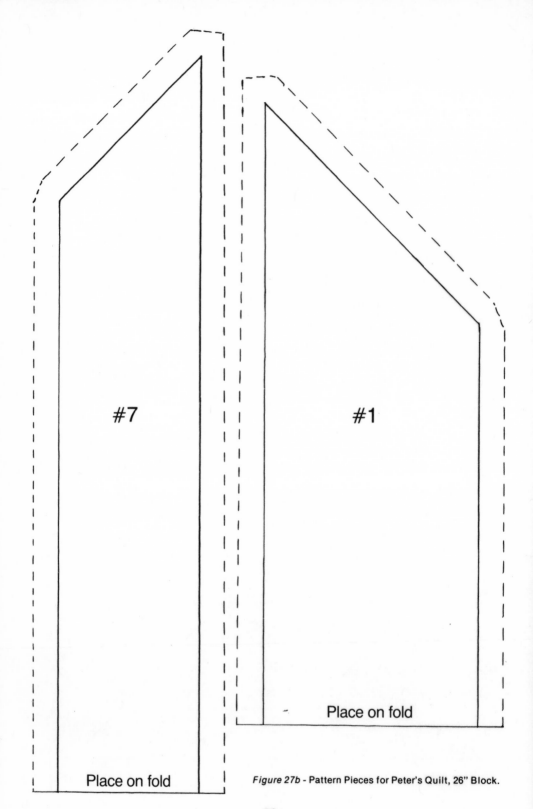

#7

Place on fold

#1

Place on fold

Figure 27b - Pattern Pieces for Peter's Quilt, 26" Block.

82

#4	8 turquoise	#5	8 turquoise	#6	8 turquoise
	5 golden orange		4 golden orange		4 golden orange
	5 medium pink		6 medium pink		4 medium pink
	4 very light pink		4 very light pink		4 very light pink
	1 light pink		1 light pink		1 light pink
	5 salmon		5 salmon		5 salmon
	4 brown		4 brown		8 brown
	4 medium blue		4 medium blue		2 medium blue

#7	8 turquoise	#8	4 turquoise
	4 golden orange		8 golden orange
	4 medium pink		8 medium pink
	4 very light pink		8 light pink
	4 light pink		8 salmon
	4 salmon		
	4 brown		
	4 medium blue		

Crosses

"Crosses", (Plate XVII) which Nancy Crow designed in 1976, is another dazzling quilt made with simple pattern pieces, which, again, could be just as easily made by the pressed quilt technique as by patchwork. It is an all-over quilt made up of nine of the blocks diagrammed in Figure 28.

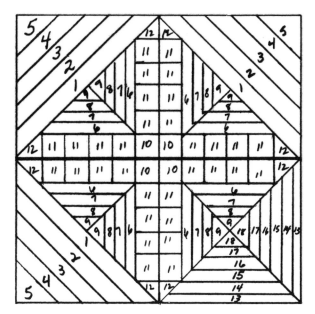

18 PATTERN PIECES

Figure 28 - Diagram for Crosses

Courtesy Nancy Crow

PLATE XVII
Crosses, designed and pieced by Nancy Crow, Athens, Ohio, 1976.

The many pattern pieces which go to make up Crosses are too large to reproduce in a book this size, even on one of our fancy fold-outs, but you can reproduce them yourself by drafting a 16" square and working from Figure 28, dividing it up as Nancy has. The entire block is a 32" square but you can work out the pattern pieces by working with only one-fourth of the block, as it repeats itself. Thus the 16" square.

DIAMONDS

The Evening Star

After the country was settled, and quiltmaking became more of a hobby than a necessity, quiltmakers started vying with one another to see who could do the smallest, daintiest work, and no pattern was more abused in this way than the Evening Star, which sometimes shows up as a motley collection of tiny stars, often as small as two inches across.

Originally, however, the Evening Star was a bold pattern, usually put together with hexagons, and there are *several surviving 18th-century Linsey-woolsey Evening Stars in private collections. We moderns are returning to our ancestor's preference for large, bold patterns, and I adapted the Evening Star Quilt in Plate XVIII from a Linsey-woolsey quilt made in New England about 1800.

I kept the scale of the 19th-century quilt, but felt I wanted the added design interest and better fabric utilization I could get by setting the stars with a log-cabin type hexagon. Directions for making these log-cabin hexagons by an easy machine method are given in Chapter VI.

The quilt in Plate XVIII was made to solve a specific problem: dark cherry (almost maroon) furniture condemned to a cold north room carpeted in bright red. I combined remnants which I found in a red to match the carpet with some in the maroon of the furniture with a heavy, fleecy maroon-and-gray plaid. Material from three gray suits discarded by husband and father provided the background. Although color contrasts might have been enough to make this quilt interesting, the added surface contrast of the pressedwork hexagons provided a great deal more interest.

When I had used up most of my reds and maroons, and could make no more stars, the quilt was still not large enough, so I made it bigger with pressed-work borders, which kept the spirit of the hexagons and added interest in their own right.

For a double-bed sized quilt like this one, you will need seven stars (made up of 42 #1 diamonds); sixteen hexagons (each with the small hexagon center given in Figure 30 if you use the log-cabin hexagons); 4 #2 setting triangles; four #3 setting triangles, and however many borders you decide to use. The pattern pieces are given in Figure 29. This makes a square quilt. The addition of three stars and two hexagons will give you a more standard shape.

If you are working with remnants and recycled garments, all of your

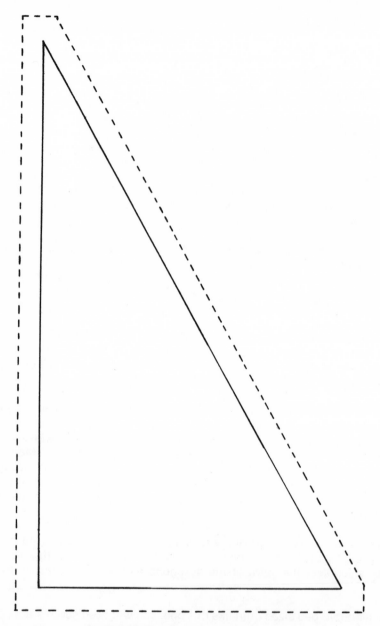

Figure 29- Pattern Piece for the Evening Star.

To make a pattern for the #1 diamond, fold a piece of typing paper, and place the base line of this triangle on the fold. This will give you half a diamond. Label the long edge "place on fold".

This pattern can also be used to draft the pattern for the #2 setting triangle. Again, fold a piece of paper, but this time put the perpendicular (the left-hand line) on the fold.

PLATE XVIII
Evening Star detail, wool with red cotton flannel backing, machine made by Jean Dubois, Durango, Colorado, 1977. This quilt was adapted from an 18th-century Linsey-woolsey quilt and set with Log-cabin hexagons.

diamonds will not be cut from the same material. You can put your darker colors in the center of the quilt and work out toward the light, or vice versa. If your materials are similar, but not identical, you might want to work them in gradually by using different materials in alternate rays of the star, as I did in the quilt pictured in Plate XVIII. I had large pieces of red and maroon wool and a small piece of a shade between the two. If I had been making each star entirely of the same material, I could not have used the small remnant at all; there was only enough to make one star, and that would have stuck out like the proverbial sore thumb. Instead, I used it in alternate rays in two stars, as well as in several hexagon centers, and the fabric then served to blend the other two reds together.

Make your stars first, getting the #1 diamond pattern by folding a piece of paper in half and putting the base of the triangle given in Figure 29 on the fold. This will give you half of a diamond (lengthwise), which is easier to use in this size than a whole one. When cutting your 42 #1 diamonds, lay the long side of this pattern on the fold.

To assemble a star, lay six diamonds out on a tabletop, points together, in a star shape. Now separate the top three from the bottom three, so that you can think of them as two different ray assemblies. Pin two of the top rays together, diamond midpoint to center star, being careful not to stretch the wool. Pin two of the bottom rays together.

Sew on the machine, setting the seam guide at ¼". Do not sew into the seam allowance at the center star end.

Now, clip threads and remove pins. About a half-inch from the center of the star, pin the seams to the left. It is better not to press them at this stage, because it is so easy to stretch wool out of shape, but you do need them out of the way. Attach the third diamond to each assembly, stitching from the star center toward the midpoint, and putting the needle in at the point where the stitching line of the first seam began.

Clip threads and again pin seam lines to the left. Lay the two assemblies together, right side to right side, and put a needle through the exact center of the middle diamond in the lower assembly, running through the exact center of the middle diamond of the upper assembly. Pin the rest of the seam. Sew, being certain that your seam line runs through the point where your shorter seam lines stopped, i.e., the exact center of the star. Press all seams to the left.

This technique of running the center seam all the way through the star helps combat the star's tendency to bunch in the middle. If your star does bunch, check your diamond pattern to be sure it is exactly true. If your star still bunches slightly in spite of all your precautions, take comfort in the knowledge that many imperfections in the patching are overcome in the quilting. Ruby McKim, in her **One Hundred and One Patchwork Patterns**, tells of a Lone Star quilt that "breezed up like a circus tent" when it went into the frame. Yet she reported that she saw it "quilt down to satisfaction".

To draft the setting hexagons, draw a 6½-inch line on a piece of tracing paper. Using the angle given in Figure 30, measure a 120° angle upward at each end of the base line and extend these new sides to 6½ inches. Connect the two sides, and you have half a hexagon. Half a hexagon is easier to work with in this size than a whole one. Pin the long side of the pattern on the crosswise fold when cutting.

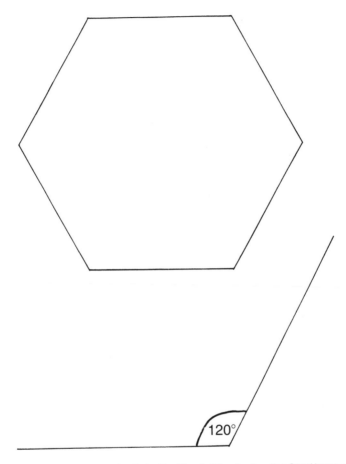

Figure 30 - Center Hexagon and Angle for Drafting Setting for Evening Star Hexagon.

Although the amount of material needed for the light and for the dark strips in the log-cabin hexagon looks about the same, less material is actually required of the first fabric applied (in this case, the plaid) than of the second. I had enough of the plaid for all sixteen hexagons, but one suit did not provide enough for all. I therefore used a dark gray suit to make the six which surround the central star, and with the help of a little astute patching (see Figure 48, Chapter VI) stretched a lighter gray suit to make the ten hexagons which form the outside edges of the quilt. That left enough dark gray for the border, and solved the problem of my pattern disappearing into the border where identical colors touched. Although this quilt can be assembled as the blocks are finished, it is perhaps better, if you are working with recycled materials and remnants, as I was, to make the final decisions about color arrangement when all the blocks are finished and can be laid out on the bed for evaluation.

When the quilt top is assembled, even it out into a perfect rectangle. If this is carefully done, this process will leave you with all but two of the necessary setting triangles. Cut the remaining two setting triangles, using the bottom half of the #1 diamond for a pattern.

If this quilt were made on a smaller scale, it would be effective as a tied quilt; however, these big pattern pieces provide scope for interesting quilting.

Although the English quilters recommend contrast as an important element in the design of the quilting, an old American adage recommends curves with curves and straight lines with straight lines, and the early 19th-century quilt which inspired me to make this Evening Star followed the American custom. It was quilted with stars within stars within stars, and hexagons within the hexagons, within the hexagons. The quilt, particularly in this log-cabin form, makes such a bold, almost masculine geometric statement, that I decided that a quilting design composed of curves and curlicues (even bold ones) would destroy the artistic integrity of the quilt.

I therefore chose to use the quilting pattern to re-enforce the structural lines of the quilt, and to use the space as a study in simplicities. I therefore filled each #1 diamond with three smaller diamonds, and each small central hexagon with another hexagon. I repeated these lines at the centers of the stars, which still needed to be fastened down in some way. When it came to the large hexagons, I decided to start by repeating their simple straight lines in the plaid sections, which had plenty of interesting surface texture of their own, and to enrich the plain sections by tying them down with French knots instead of quilting them. Quilting in the narrow border strips follows the structural lines.

I did the quilting (except for the French knots, of course) by machine, partly to prove that it could be done, and partly because this was intended to be a utility quilt in a boy's room, and I wanted it to be sturdy enough for hard use and frequent washing. The lines of the quilting are much harder and sharper than they would have been had I quilted by hand but for that reason they re-enforce the bold geometrics of the quilt, and are equally effective if not more so.

Machine Quilting

Most machine quilters recommend loosening the tension on the bobbin thread, and if you have one of those marvelous new sewing machines, that of course is the best way to do it. With my old clunker, however, I have to adjust the bobbin tension with a screwdriver, and every time I fool with it, it gets so out of whack that it costs me $15 to have it professionally adjusted. I've discovered, from talking with other seamstresses, that most machines **are** this way, and so have experimented endlessly with finding ways to machine-quilt with a less-than-perfect machine.

And it **is** possible. Set your stitch at eight, with normal tension. Test on a sample - and I mean a sample that has the lining, interlining, etc. in it - to make sure that your stitch is perfectly adjusted so that it is the same on both front and back. Your machine handbook will illustrate this and tell you how to accomplish it. OR take it to a repairman, and pay your $15 cheerfully. Your stitch **has** to be perfect. Loops and snags on the backside are going to look terrible on a quilt, and can't be tolerated.

Pin every quarter-inch along the quilting line, at right angles to the line. I know this is a prodigious number of pins, but it's easier to pin than to baste, particularly on a long piece. In theory, it would be more efficient to pin large areas at a time, but in practice the pins fall out or get stuck on things as the quilt is maneuvered in and out of the machine, and I have found it better in the long run to pin one continuous quilting line at a time, whether it be a four-foot border line or a two-inch diamond. I run my thread ends into a needle and hide them in the batting as I go along, just as I do for hand quilting.

Both in the pinning and in the sewing, it is best to start in the middle and work outward, so that if there is extra fullness, it will be smoothed out and off the edge of the quilt. However, this is taking on the hardest part first, and you may find that discouraging. It is fairly easy to do the quilting along the edges of the quilt, but getting that enormous bulk into place in order to quilt the center section is a little like trying to put a patch on the knee of a size three overall. You might be better off to do a few of the edge motifs first, to convince yourself that you **can** do machine quilting, before you tackle the center sections. Or machine-quilt a crib quilt your first time out.

When sewing, keep both palms flat on the surface, exerting a gentle pressure outward, to keep the fabric absolutely flat while stitching. If the work begins to hang up on a seam or a pin, push gently away from you, to help the machine keep on at the same rate of speed. This will not only help prevent puckering, but will keep the stitch of an even length.

It is much easier, of course, to do machine stitching by the apartment method, one block or section at a time, so that you don't have the entire bulk of the quilt to cope with, but it is perfectly possible to do an entire quilt at once. If you're doing an entire quilt, however, be sure to work on a large tabletop, so that as much of the quilt as possible lies on the table while you work. Otherwise, the weight of the quilt pulls so heavily on the stitching being done that it is impossible to keep the stitch length even. I also keep an extra chair next to my own so that it can help support the weight of the part of the quilt that isn't on the tabletop or in my lap.

CURVES

Wool adapts better to curves than cotton does and when you are working with a patchwork pattern which includes a curved seam, you are better off working in wool than in cotton. Here, wool's stretchiness, instead of being a disadvantage to the quiltmaker, as it is along straight bias pieces, is an advantage. Wool adjusts itself to a curve, and provides a neater, flatter finish all along it than cotton does.

Rob Peter to Pay Paul

Of all the traditional curved patterns, Rob Peter to Pay Paul is the simplest and the most popular. Rob Peter to Pay Paul is a counterchange design, a design technique borrowed from the ornamental artists of antiquity. Perhaps, like so many other ancient designs, this one came home to northern Europe with the returning crusaders, who had seen it during their travels on a near-eastern tiled floor or garden wall. A counterchange design is a simple thing. It is made, as the name of this family of quilt patterns implies, by cutting identical shapes out of a black square and a white square and then "robbing" the black cutout from the black square and inserting it into the white square, and vice versa.

All of the patterns in this Rob Peter to Pay Paul family are created by using two simple basic repeat units (Figure 31) combined in various ways. Since the size of the repeat unit affects the appearance of the pattern in such a basic way, and since it is so easy to draft, I have not limited your possibilities by giving a pattern. Simply draft a true square, and, putting the point of your compass in one corner, mark off a curved line. How big the quarter-circle that you remove from the square is, of course, will also have a tremendous effect on the appearance of your repeat unit and therefore of the finished quilt. Your curved line should intersect the base line of the square about two-thirds of the way across, as in Figure 31.

Figure 31 - Repeat units, Rob Peter to Pay Paul.

Even when we use a pattern that has been used by generations of women before us, our finished quilts - because of our choice of color and materials, because of the size of our blocks, because of the way we design the set and the quilting - are unique. I think that is one of the enduring joys and values of quiltmaking, and it holds true even when we use the simplest of patterns. There are a large number of traditional patchwork patterns that have remained popular down through the generations because of their simplicity. Others, like Rob Peter to Pay Paul, the Log Cabins, and the Grandmother's Fan patterns, although not as simple to construct, remain best-sellers because of their flexibility. There is almost no end to the number of ways the repeat units of these patterns can be set together.

The basic Rob Peter to Pay Paul (Figure 32a), perhaps the most common combination, is a self-contained, dazzling, all-over pattern. The repeat units, however, can also be combined into vine-like designs like the Vine of Friendship (Figure 32b) which takes off diagonally across the quilt; or like Falling Timbers (Figure 32c) which creates a vine-like trellis.

a   Rob Peter to Pay Paul

b   Vine of Friendship

c   Falling Timbers

d   Fool's Puzzle

Figure 32 - Common Settings, Rob Peter to Pay Paul

PLATE XIX
Rob Peter to Pay Paul, Love Ring Variation, Amish, Lancaster County, Pennsylvania, c. 1900.

Collection of Barbara S. Janos and Barbara Ross, New York City

94

Wonder of the World creates an isolated stylized flower, while Fool's Puzzle (Figure 32d), to my mind a far more interesting block, connects its stylized flowers with black squares.

Drunkard's Path, perhaps the most commonly seen of the vine-type arrangements, sometimes differs from the others in its use of a third color.

These repeat units can also be arranged, much as the Log Cabin Barn-Raising quilt is arranged, so that they form concentric circles. This arrangement, called Love Ring or Nonesuch, frees the pattern from the bondage of light and dark, and even from the three-color format of Drunkard's Path, and permits it to be expressed in any range of colors the quiltmaker wishes to use. Plate XIX shows a magnificent Amish interpretation of this pattern.

All of these patterns sometimes go under the name of Rob Peter to Pay Paul. All the vine-type arrangements are sometimes called the Drunkard's path. Most have several other names as well, so I have solved the problem by borrowing my nomenclature from Carrie Hall, as I usually do when confronted with difficulty in naming a quilt*

Grandmother's Fan

Grandmother's Fan patterns - along with other representational designs like butterflies and little red schoolhouses - began to be popular about the time of the war between the states. Fans, because they provided (in their spokes) an interesting outlet for small scraps left over from other projects and because there were so many interesting ways to set the blocks together, remained popular and, in fact, became almost a craze during the 1870's and 1880's, when they were taken up by the Victorians, who used them as samplers for the display of exotic materials and fancy embroidery (see Chapter VII).

The pattern for the basic fan is given in Figure 33. This pattern makes a 10" square. For each block, you need to cut:

7 #1 spokes   1 #2 quarter-circle   1 #3 background

Generally speaking, it is a good idea to use your more aggressive colors in the spokes, and a dark color in the #2 quarter-circles. So many wool Grandmother's Fan quilts used black for this quarter-circle that black has become almost obligatory. Historically, the #3 background piece was cut from a neutral color, but dazzling Grandmother Fan quilts can be created with the use of a dark color in the background, and the possibility should not be overlooked. It is more important, I think, to find a color available in enough quantity to use in all the blocks, so that the background of the individual fan blocks can tie the quilt together visually. It is also important, when choosing the material for this pattern piece, to remember that whatever fancy quilting you decide to do will be mostly on this material. If you plan to do hand quilting, be especially careful to pick a wool which has a crisp enough surface to show off your quilting. If you have

*Hall, Carrie A., and Rose G. Kretsinger, **The Romance of the Patchwork Quilt in America**. Although written in 1935, this book is still the standard reference book in the field.

never quilted on wool before, you may want to experiment a bit. There are wools - usually the soft, stretchy ones (but fleecy surfaces too) which absorb the quilting stitches, and these wools are better used for tied or pressed quilts where their texture does not present a problem.

To make a sample block:

1. Sew the seven #1 spokes together, keeping all the narrow ends at one end. Press.
2. Sew the #2 quarter-circle along the narrow end of the assembled spokes. Clip the seam and press.
3. Sew the #3 background along the wide end of the spokes. Clip the seam and press.

Grandmother's Fan can be set with alternate plain blocks or with lattice strips of various kinds, but it was traditionally used as an all-over design. Plate XX illustrates the most common set, and other favorite sets are illustrated in Figure 34.

Figure 34 - Common Settings for Grandmother's Fan.

PLATE XX
Detail, Grandmother's Fan, made by Mrs. S.R. Sherwin, Harvard, Nebraska, c. 1897. The fans are identical, the colors on all the spokes progressing alike: grey-green; bright blue; tan; red; tan; bright blue; grey-green. The background is an extremely dark brown, and the feather stitching is done throughout in a glossy single-strand yellow embroidery floss. The backing is an elegant brown cotton brocade. The ties are narrow lemon-yellow ribbons.

Courtesy Mrs. Thomas B. Johnson, Seward, Nebraska

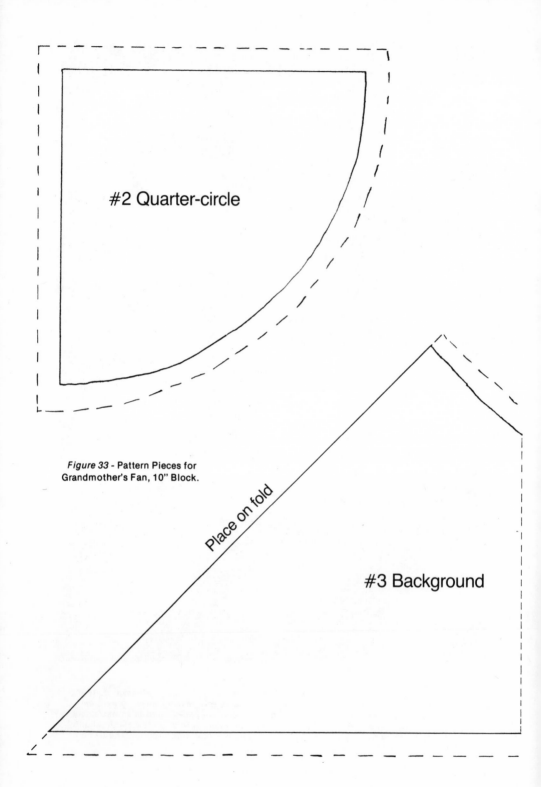

#2 Quarter-circle

Place on fold

#3 Background

Figure 33 - Pattern Pieces for
Grandmother's Fan, 10" Block.

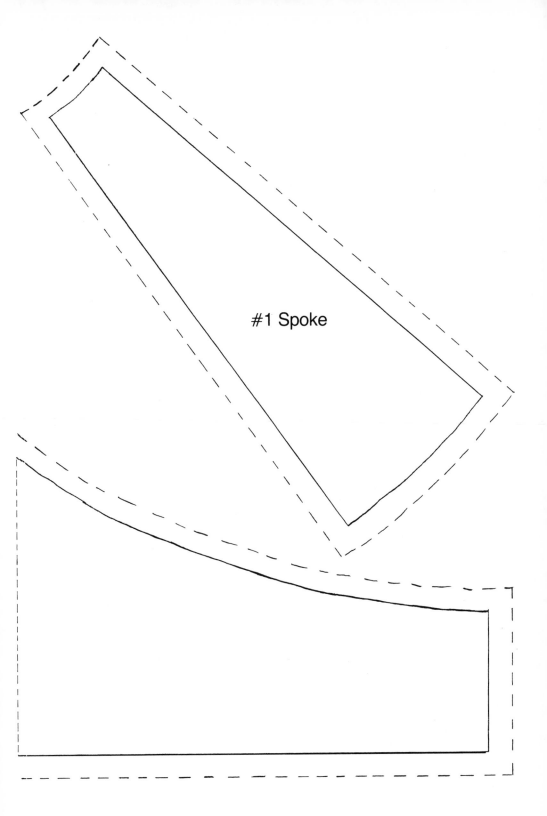

#1 Spoke

If the #2 quarter-circle and the two outside #1 spokes are pieced in the same color in every block, and the blocks are then set diagonally, the pattern will make its own extremely effective latticework. The setting triangles of the quilt made necessary by the diagonal set could then be done in the color of the latticework in order to provide a border for the quilt.

Like Rob Peter to Pay Paul, the Grandmother's Fan block can be set in the Love Ring pattern as illustrated in Plate XXI. If you wish to use this set, it will be necessary to cut both the #2 and #3 pieces of the same color. In this quilt, which is a cotton quilt, various black fabrics are used in the background, and the spokes are jewelled tones. Each square is decorated with an overcast looped embroidery stitch and each patch, within each square, is also decorated with the same stitch.

Historically, fan quilts have been made with small blocks, possibly so that the individual spokes could use the really tiny pieces left over from other projects, but a dazzling modern quilt could be made from this pattern using large blocks. For instance, a king-size quilt like the one in Figure 35 could be made using only eight fan blocks, eight plain blocks, and a border. Doubling the width of the top and bottom borders provides a more practical shape for the quilt than leaving it square.

Figure 35 - Grandmother's Fan, Whole Quilt Design.

PLATE XXI
Grandmother's Fan, Love Ring Setting, all cotton, collected in Pennsylvania.

To draft the pattern for this quilt decide first on the size square you want to use. Get the quarter-circle by putting the point of your compass in one corner. The second curved line will be more difficult, as your compass leg isn't long enough to stretch. Women out on the old frontier solved this one by tying a piece of string to a pencil and holding the string down with a thumb when their "compass" was in use.

Grandmother's Fan quilts, like Plate XX, are frequently tied, but there is no reason why they can't be quilted, and they often are. The spokes of the fan are usually quilted ¼" inside the seam line to re-enforce this strong design element. The #2 and #3 spaces are often filled with curves within curves, echoing the structural line of the pattern piece. The quilt in Plate XXI, however, achieves an interesting contrast to this long curved line by echoing the square lines instead. Both are easily marked and quickly made. Other, more intricate patterns can fill the space, however, and Marie Graeff pictures a beautiful fan quilt in which a fleur-de-lis fills this space.*

The Japanese Fan, an interesting applique adaptation of the Dresden Plate pattern so popular in the 1930's and 1940's into the fan format is given in Chapter V.

*Graeff, Marie Knorr, Pennsylvania German Quilts, p. 10.

CHAPTER 5

APPLIQUE QUILTS

Although patchwork has eclipsed applique in contemporary work, applique and patchwork techniques were equally common in 18th-century quilts. Technically, applique is easier than patchwork. It requires only the knowledge of how to get a seam allowance to fold under smoothly, even on the most difficult shapes; of how to get the design applied exactly where it is supposed to be; and of how to slide a blind-stitch under the edge of the pattern piece being applied to the quilttop.* In addition, applique does not require the precision in pattern-making and cutting required in patchwork. However, the design of the applique quilt, because applique work is more fluid and more flexible than patchwork, is more difficult and challenging.

Traditional applique quilts are whole-cloth quilts; i.e., the pattern pieces are applied onto a foundation which **is** the quilttop. Since 1800, however, many, if not most, applique quilts have been made by the block method.

During the 19th century block applique quilts were so often set with alternate white blocks that the resulting tedium almost discredited the applique method. There are interesting and creative ways to set applique blocks, however, and of course we modern workers have a fabulous palette of fast colors at our fingertips, and no longer have to depend so heavily on white for a safe set.

There are other interesting ways to deal with applique blocks, however. One of these is the use, in the same quilt, of two different blocks which compliment each other. A traditional quilt of this type is the Lotus quilt, in which a lotus bud block alternates with a lotus flower block. Other applique blocks, particularly those which are based on an X, can be set together all-over, and often create unexpectedly interesting patterns where the blocks come together. A good example is the Laurel Leaf Quilt in Plate XXIV.

Even when they are set together all-over, some applique blocks - particularly blossoms and wreaths - tend to stay in the center of their blocks, and the result is a series of unrelated motifs. One historic solution to this problem was filling up the empty space with intricate quilting, particularly stuffed quilting, which has equal visual impact with the applique. The success of this method is attested to by the many breath-taking examples now hanging in our museums. Another solution is the inclusion of a leaf or bud sprig in the corners of the blocks, designed to combine with the sprigs in the corners of the contiguous blocks.

*Many workers both historically and contemporaneously, have scorned the blind stitch (which is easier and almost invisible) and used instead a sturdy but dainty hemming stitch.

Early twentieth-century quilt designers, of whom Anne Orr was the most creative, experimented with varying the size and shape of the blocks, proving that we don't have to give up flexibility in design in exchange for the convenience of the block technique. She illustrated in her work that an individual applique quilt can have several sizes of blocks. A typical Anne Orr quilt, for instance, displays the central motif in a large central panel which is surrounded by corner squares and rectangular panels which restate that motif. Several borders of different widths usually frame the design. So the ground has been broken for creative work in applique, and I think it is only a matter of time before contemporary quiltmakers will work in applique and patchwork with equal enthusiasm.

Wool quilts made with applique techniques are few and far between, partly, I think, because the crisp look we associate with applique is impossible to obtain with wool. More important, perhaps, is the fact that applique quilts, through some fluke of historical destiny, have come to be thought of as "company" quilts (i.e., bedspreads), rather than utility quilts. Because it stretches easily, particularly on the bias, however, wool is in some ways better adapted to applique than cotton is, and the possibilities of wool applique should not be overlooked.

I may have mentioned on twelve or thirteen previous occasions that there are some difficulties in working with wool. One of these - the fact that wool will not take a sharp crease easily - is of particular importance when doing applique work. Normally, the best approach in applique is to cut out the pattern piece, clip the curves, place a cardboard template (which is the exact duplicate of the pattern) on top of the pattern piece and then press the seam allowance back on top of the template. When you try this with wool, however, you'll find that you are mostly steaming your fingers, and that not much else is happening.

The solution - or the one I decided worked best after a trial-and-error session with several other techniques - is to pin the pattern piece to a **paper** template and **baste** the seam allowances back (through the paper template). Press from both the right and wrong sides, pull out the basting threads and remove the paper. Pin the finished pattern pieces in place before the creases decide to disappear.

In the old days, many quiltmakers (particularly in England) left their papers in place, and it is by these papers that some old quilts have been dated. For a quilt which is occasionally going to need washing, however, papers should not be left in place, as they will bunch up when they get wet.

Precision cutting is not necessary in applique as it is in patchwork because the pattern pieces are given their final shape by the template when the seam allowance is turned back over it.

Roses and Buds

Another reason applique has been less popular than patchwork, I think, is that traditionally applique quilts have been rich women's quilts. The fabric is bought especially for the quilt. It is all the same. There is no demonstration of a problem solved or of difficulties overcome. This doesn't have to be so, however. The Roses and Buds quilt (sometimes called Combination Rose) in Plate XXII which I made for my daughter Chris from a pattern popular in the 1850's made extensive use of remnants and recycled materials.

I was able to cut sixteen squares plus a number of one-fourth-sized squares from a dark brown remnant. I used twelve of these squares for the applique blocks, and put the other four at the corners of the quilt. I used the small squares to extend various browns cut from old suits of which Chris' father & grandfather donated. I cut these suits entirely into 6" blocks, because there are few spots in a man's suit from which a 12" block can come, and I also felt that by cutting them smaller and spreading them around, they fit into the background surface better than larger squares of various browns would.

The light gold of the roses I picked up at a summer sale, the dark gold was a damaged remnant which I got at half the sale price, and the green was left over from another quilt.

Because my daughter lives in Seattle, away from our vicious winters, I backed the quilt in cotton flannel rather than wool and didn't interline it at all, so it wouldn't be too warm to use.

The pattern pieces given in Figure 36 produce a 12" block, which when assembled as in the quilt in Plate XXII provide a twin-bed quilt 60" x 84" in which the pattern will cover the top of the bed and allow a one-block (12") plain overhang. If you want a double-bed size using this set, use the patterns in Figure 37, which produce a 15" block, and plan to use four applique blocks across and five up. (That counts corners twice, of course). For a larger, Queen-size or King-size bed using this type of set, you will want to consider a central motif as well, perhaps a block of six appliqued squares, or a fabulous quilted central medallion.

Trace the pattern pieces from Figure 36 (putting the #1 rose on the fold), and transfer them to cardboard with carbon paper to make your pattern templates. You will use these templates to make the paper patterns for cutting and for shaping the pattern pieces later. Before you start to cut your fabric, check out your pattern pieces. Draft a 12½" square on heavy paper. Postal wrapping paper works well. Fold it in half diagonally both ways, and then fold it in half vertically **and** horizontally. Cut out your cardboard templates and trace them onto your paper square to make sure that the pattern works, and also to see whether you prefer the pattern set straight or diagonally. Trace it one way on one side of the paper, lining the flatter sides of the roses (where the buds attach) up with the diagonal folds on one side of the paper, and with the horizontal and vertical folds on the other side. It may help to punch a hole in the exact center of your #1 rose to help in getting it at the exact center of the block, where all the folds intersect. Save this drawing. You will need it later on to make your placement template.

Now, trace around your 12½" square on cardboard to make the cutting template for your blocks. If you are using recycled materials, you will also need a 6½" cardboard square to cut your quarter-size blocks.

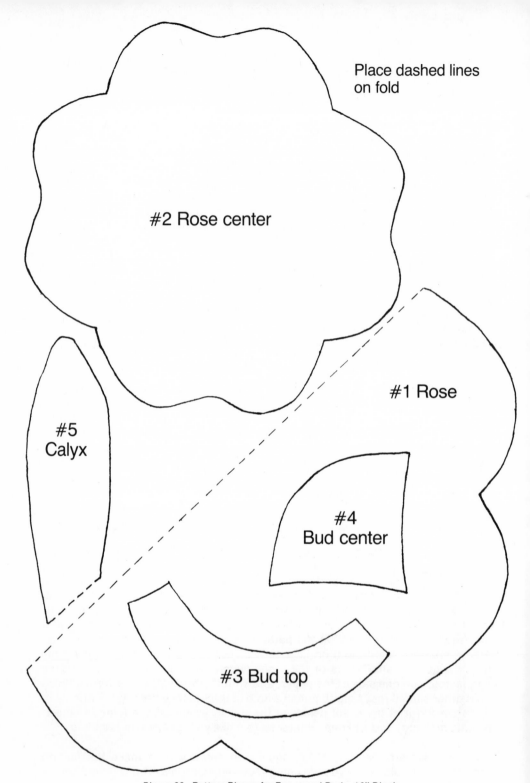

Place dashed lines
on fold

#2 Rose center

#5
Calyx

#1 Rose

#4
Bud center

#3 Bud top

Figure 36 - Pattern Pieces for Roses and Buds, 12" Block.

106

PLATE XXII
Roses and Buds applique, wool on wool, made by Jean Dubois, Durango, Colorado 1976.

Courtesy Christine Dubois, Seattle, Washington

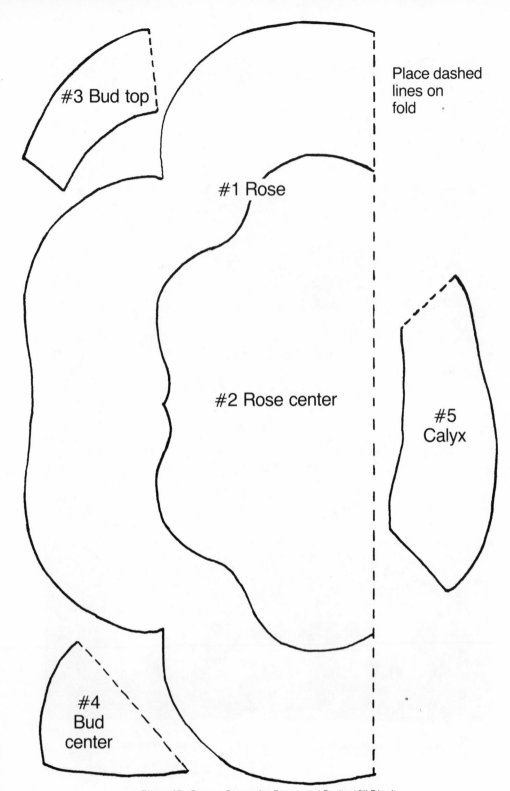

Place dashed
lines on
fold

#3 Bud top

#1 Rose

#2 Rose center

#5
Calyx

#4
Bud
center

Figure 37 - Pattern Pieces for Roses and Buds, 15" Block.

If you wish to make the twin-bed quilt in Plate XXII, you will need 12 applique blocks and 23 plain blocks. Each applique block requires:

1 #1 rose, light gold
1 #2 rose center, dark gold
4 #3 bud tops, light gold
4 #4 bud centers, dark gold
4 #5 calyxes, green

The four corner blocks are reversed in color, and each requires:

1 #1 rose, dark gold
1 #2 rose center, light gold
4 #3 bud tops, dark gold
4 #4 bud centers, light gold
4 #5 calyxes, green

Remember to allow ¼" seam allowance by eye when cutting.

While it takes a lot of clipping to get cotton to conform to circular shapes, wool adapts to them naturally, and little clipping is required. A snip at the center of the inside curve of the #3 bud top, and another on the inside of the #5 calyx where the lobes come together is all that is necessary.

On the surface of things, it seems like a lot of extra work, but in the long run it is easier to make a number of paper patterns for each pattern piece. Use these paper patterns first for cutting out the pieces, remembering to allow a ¼" seam allowance by eye when cutting. Leave them in place until you have turned under the seam allowances and basted them down, through the paper pattern. Press and remove stitches. The paper pattern can then be used again for a cutting pattern.

Turn under the edges of the #1 rose, the #2 rose center and the #5 calyx as described, or by some other method you have found workable. The #3 bud top needs turning under only on the curved edges, and the #4 bud center can be used flat, as is.

To make the rose assembly, place the smaller rose in the exact center of the large one. Pin at frequent intervals and stitch it down. Your stitches will be less visible if you use a thread which exactly matches the top fabric, in this case the #2 rose center. For variety, I did not place all my center roses exactly the same way but I was careful to put them in the exact center.

To make the bud assemblies, first pin and stitch the #3 bud top to the #4 bud center. Then add the #5 calyx.

Press the background block thoroughly, but don't press the rose and rosebud assemblies, now or later. Pressing applique after the stitching is done, particularly in wool, only serves to emphasize the seam allowances.

With a big block like this one, it is easier to make a placement template than to mark the exact diagonals of each block, trace the patterns on, etc. Instead, use your 12½" square paper pattern. Cut it in half along one of the diagonal folds. Then cut out the rose and buds from one half. This is your block placement template. It should look like Figure 38.

Figure 38 - Placement Template, Roses and Buds.

To use the placement template, pin it securely to the fabric block. Pin the center of the rose assembly in place first, then pin the centers of the three bud assemblies which are included on your template. Remove template to the other half of the block, or place the final bud assembly in place by eye.

Now, pin the center rose assembly down thoroughly, remembering that liberal use of pins now will prevent irritating problems later. Be careful not to stretch either the finished assemblies or the block in the process. Now sew down the rose.

Make whatever minor adjustments are necessary in placement of the buds, pin them down thoroughly, and sew them to the background block. When you come to the spot between the two lobes of the calyx, where the seam had to be slit to make the seam allowance turn under smoothly, re-enforce the seam with tiny overcast stitches.

The Laurel Leaf Quilt

Needless to say, I made the Roses and Buds quilt to prove that applique can be done in wool. Now that we're past that stage, let's give some thought to the possibilities of other favorite applique patterns. The Laurel Leaf, another block pattern, is interesting because it illustrates the success possible with a severely restricted number of pattern pieces - three leaves and a stem. The Shelburne Laurel Leaf in Plate XXIV, as a matter of fact, uses only two leaves and a stem.

Even though we in the United States have always been wary about having royalty of our own, we have an exaggerated interest in other people's royalty and all their doings. Napoleon, Emperor of France, was no exception. During the early 19th century, the young Republic took to the styles of the French court, particularly the Empire (pronounced ahm-**peer**) furniture and the exaggeratedly high empire waistlines of the French ladies' dresses, which were designed to make them look as if they were about to provide the emperor with a new crop of soldiers for his conquest of Europe.

The Laurel Leaf*, borrowed from the Romans, and symbolic of the conqueror's crown, is a Napoleonic design element which, when adapted into a quilt block, was popular throughout the nineteenth century. It was frequently used, as Rebexy Gray Hamilton used it, in alternate blocks (Plate XXIII), but it also made a dazzling all-over quilt, particularly when the color arrangement was designed, as in Plate XXIV, so that floral motifs were emphasized where the blocks came together. It would also be interesting, I think, set like the Roses and Buds quilt in Plate XXII, and bordered like an Amish quilt.

Pattern pieces for a Laurel Leaf quilt are given in Figure 39. There are three sizes of leaves given in the pattern, so you can vary your laurel sprig to suit your own taste. To make a sample 12" block using all three sizes of leaves, with the color scheme used in the Shelburne Quilt, you will need to cut:

4 #1 leaves, light blue
8 #2 leaves, light blue
24 #3 leaves, dark blue
2 stems, dark blue

Laurel leaves are more difficult to construct than more rounded leaf shapes are, but this really no problem when you work with wool, especially if you cut on the bias. Start by cutting a number of light cardboard templates for each leaf size. Index cards are a good weight cardboard for this job.

A true pattern is hard to get by tracing on wool, so don't try to trace around

*Better known on kitchen shelves as Bay Leaf.

PLATE XXIII
Detail, Laurel Leaf Quilt made by Rebexy Gray Hamilton of Waynesburg,
Pennsylvania, c. 1850. Note the effective contrast provided by the patchwork sawtooth
border, and the repetition of the X-shape of the laurel in the feather quilting of the
alternate blocks.

PLATE XXIV
Laurel Leaf Quilt, all-over set, third quarter nineteenth century.

Courtesy Shelburne Museum, Inc., Shelburne, Vermont

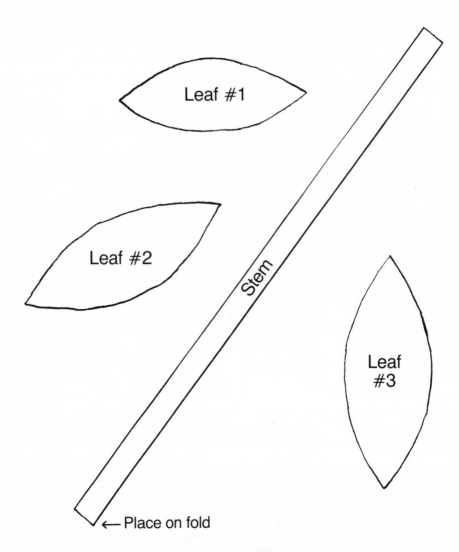

Leaf #1

Leaf #2

Stem

Leaf #3

← Place on fold

Figure 39 - Pattern Pieces for Laurel Leaf Quilt, 12" Block.

the template to cut out your leaves. Rather, pin the leaf template to the wool and cut around it, leaving ¼" seam allowance by eye as you cut. This cut-out leaf should look like Figure 40a.

Because the wool will stretch enough, no clipping of curves need be done before turning under the seam allowance. While the leaf is still pinned to the template, turn the seam allowance down over onto the top of the cardboard, and, using a thread that matches the wool as exactly as possible, baste the leaf into the shape of the template. To do this, turn the seam allowance down over the top point first, as in Figure 40b. Bring the seam allowances from first one side and then the other over on top of the template to form a perfect point, and baste it firmly in place. Now run a running stitch down along the side of the leaf, pulling it only tightly enough to give the wool the shape of the template. Do **not** baste through the cardboard, as you will want to remove it and use it again. Form the second point as you did the first one, and then baste down along the other edge. The finished leaf should look like Figure 40d.

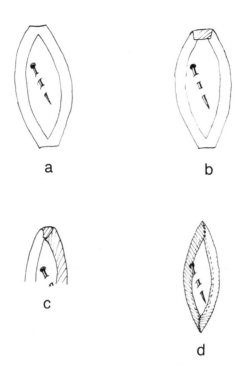

a   b

c

d

Figure 40 - Applique Technique: Construction of a Laurel Leaf

Remove the pin, but leave the template in place until you have pressed the leaf with a steam iron and have let it dry thoroughly. The basting stitches will not show, and there is no reason to remove them.

The stems are easier to prepare, because their ends will be tucked under a laurel leaf and need no finishing.

Now, cut your foundation block, adding the seam allowance.

Next, make a cardboard template like the one in Figure 41. If you are designing your block to make use of leaves #1 and #2 only, you can trace Figure 41 as it is; otherwise, fold a paper square the size of the foundation block in half diagonally, twice. Lay the stems, and then the laurel leaves in position along the stems in an attractive pattern, pin them down, and then trace around them. This is your placement template.

Figure 41 - Laurel Leaf Placement Template

116

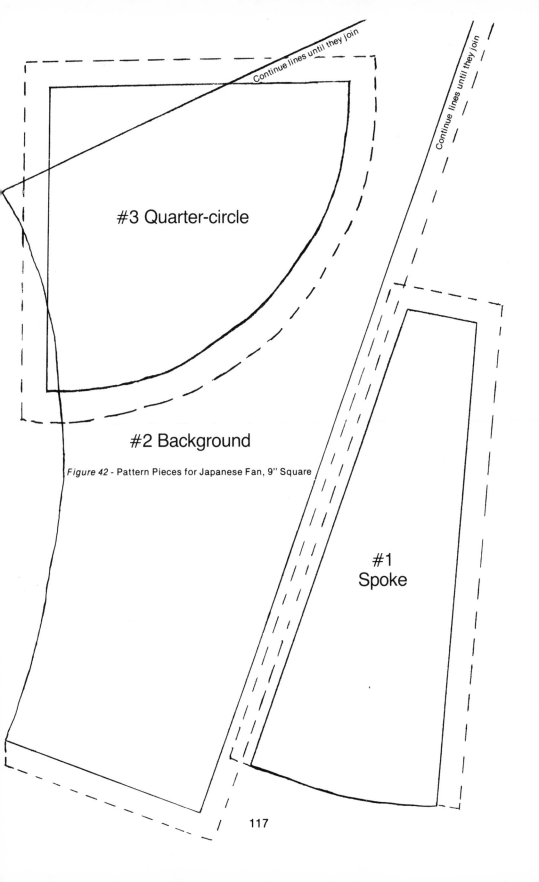

Continue lines until they join

Continue lines until they join

#3 Quarter-circle

#2 Background

Figure 42 - Pattern Pieces for Japanese Fan, 9" Square

#1
Spoke

This template will help you position your patterns perfectly on every block, and will save hours of needless frustration. Needless to say, the effectiveness of a quilt like the one in Plate XXIII would be completely destroyed if the laurel blocks were not identical. To use the template, first draw the diagonals for the stems in chalk, with a ruler, or fold and press your foundation block diagonally in each direction to get these marks. Using your template, mark the design on the foundation block with chalk. Position the template by putting the stem end in the exact center of the block and centering the bud end on the diagonal line. Repeat three times on each block. Your template should be made slightly smaller than the pattern, so the chalk won't show once the leaves are in place.

Now you are ready to assemble your block. Pin your stems down along the diagonal folds first, putting the exact center of each stem on the exact center of the diagonal line. Now pin each leaf in place, using your chalk lines as guides, and attach the leaves with a tiny hemming stitch or a hidden catch stitch.

The Japanese Fan

It is often possible to get interesting effects by a combination of patchwork and applique, and the Japanese Fan responds particularly well to a combined approach. To make a sample block, cut a muslin foundation piece 9½" square. Plan your colors, and then cut (from wool) six #1 spokes and one each of the #2 background and the #3 quarter circle given in Figure 42.

To make the pointed Dresden spokes, fold each spoke vertically and pin the

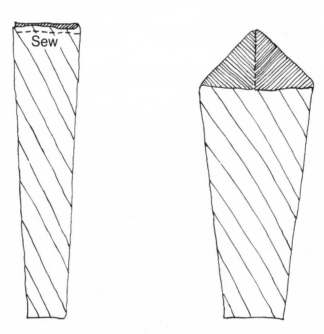

Figure 43 - Construction of a Dresden-type Fan Spoke

118

top together as in Figure 43. Sew, allowing ¼" seam allowance, kite-tail fashion for better utilization of time and thread.

Clip, turn rightside out, with the seam down the middle of the back as in Figure 43, and press.

Combine the spokes into a fan, still using a ¼" seam allowance.

In theory, you wouldn't need a backing square for applique, but with this pattern, every block will be a different size if you don't use one. Pin the #2 backing at close intervals along two of the outside edges of the backing square. Machine-baste 1/8" from the edge. If you are using heavy, soft wool, you may have trouble with stretching and puckering. Place your pins closer together, or use a roller foot as you do with knits. Or do both.

Place the pieced fan over the #2 background, making sure that the pointed Dresden tips cover the raw edges of the #2 background, and pin in place beginning with the outside spokes. Make sure both outside spokes are pinned to the edge of the backing square along their entire lengths before pinning the points of the other spokes.

Press or baste your #3 quarter-circle along the curve over a cardboard template made from the #3 pattern minus the seam allowance. Pin the #3 quarter-circle in place, over the raw edges of the spokes, first pinning its straight edges to the edges of the backing square.

Machine-baste the remaining two sides of the square. Sew all elements in place, either by hand blind-stitching or by machine top-stitching, basting first if you feel insecure about pin-basting.

Turn to the wrong side and trim any wool overlap even with the cotton backing square.

If you are what Ruby McKim used to refer to, back in the 1920's, as "a busy modern woman", you might want to machine-quilt each block as you go along by the quilt-as-you-go method. This would eliminate the necessity of sewing all the elements in place after the pinning stage. Top-stitch the fan and the #3 quarter-circle to the block, using 1/8" seam allowance. Fill in each spoke by quilting ¼" inside the seam lines. Fill in the #2 and #3 spaces with curves within curves, ½" apart. Keep your lines continuous even where interrupted by the points, although not quilting over the spokes. Again, if #2 is cut from a super-stretchy wool, you can be in trouble. Use lots of pins and a roller foot.

It is a difficult problem to draw these quilting lines in by hand with a pencil. Use dressmaker's chalk instead, installed in a dime-store compass, or make cardboard templates off the curved edges of pattern pieces #2 and #3.

For other methods of constructing fan blocks, see Chapters IV and VI, and be sure to read the discussion on fan sets in Chapter IV while you are still in the planning stage.

Designing and Marking the Quilting

If you don't think of yourself as one of McKim's busy modern women, and want to quilt on a frame, this is the moment to start thinking about designing and marking your quilting.

The first thing you need to do, when designing the quilting for a finished top, whether it be patchwork or applique, is to spread the top out somewhere where you can really look at it. Try to figure out what the quilt is trying to say, how it says it. Your quilting design should re-enforce the patchwork or applique design, or echo it, or at least not contradict it.* If there are strong patchwork or applique motifs, it is often the best idea to repeat them in the quilting, usually by quilting ¼" in from the seam line. In applique, it is often possible to quilt ¼" **out** from the seam line as well, and as a matter of fact in Hawaiian quilts that **is** the quilting design - a series of quilting lines undulating outward from each major design unit.

While you are thinking about design, think too about the **purpose** of quilting. One of the purposes of quilting is to hold the three layers of the quilt - the top, the back, and the lining - together firmly enough that it will stay together through hard wear and constant washing for several lifetimes. So, obviously, we have to fill **all** the space. That used to mean that no more than one square inch of surface could go unquilted. Now, with the synthetic battings, spaces two or three times that large can be left empty IF in so doing we do not destroy our design. For another, equally important purpose of quilting (particularly the background quilting) is to create beauty by pointing up the basic design.

When we mark a design on the quilt top, it's the line of the drawing - the proposed quilting line - that makes the design. However, in the finished quilt, it is not the line of quilting that makes the design, but the play of light on the unquilted surfaces. This has particular relevance in the design of whole-cloth quilted counterpanes, but it is equally important in the design of quilting for alternate squares, and for large background spaces in applique. Draw a Prince's Plume (see Chapter II for directions) on a piece of typing paper. Back it with parallel lines drawn by tracing along both sides of your ruler. What's wrong? The background lines are supposed to emphasize the feather, but instead they compete with it. Now, insert a line in between every two parallels on your drawing. See how that makes the feather pop out? Now the feather, which is intended to be the focus of interest, catches your eye, and the background (unless by some mischance your lines aren't parallel and demand attention for that reason) has retreated.

This is because the design of a quilted surface is created by the play of light across the **unquilted** portions of the fabric, and not by the lines of quilting themselves. And I think this is the point at which modern quilters have lost their way. In the old days, when wool or cotton batts were used, close quilting was necessary to keep the batt from bunching up. Quilting lines had to be close

---

*Not all contemporary workers agree with me. The Gutcheons (see **The Quilt Design Workbook**, pp. 160-3, strive to complement, rather than re-enforce, the design statement of the patchwork, and their approach has a validity we should at least be aware of.

together to perform their basic function of holding the top, the batt and the lining together effectively.

Nowadays, however, with synthetic batts, close quilting is no longer necessary, and - although we are still using the traditional patterns - we are leaving large areas of the background unquilted. This makes the background, which is receiving more light than the unquilted areas of the basic design, compete with the quilted design. By forgetting that the function of quilting is to create beauty by pointing up the design, as well as to hold the three layers together, modern quilters are destroying the effectiveness of an ancient art.

At the time the American colonies were being settled, the women in England marked their own quilting designs with chalk or pencil (or with the large end of a tapestry needle), using templates to mark the main outlines, and filling in the details freehand. They knew exactly how much space each unit would take so they could mark the general outlines of the patterns as they went along. For this reason, they did not mark the entire top before putting it in the frame as we do, but marked the design a section at a time as the work progressed, even on symmetrical, all-over patterns like the Welsh framed medallions. If they were working on patchwork, they usually put the quilt into the frame lining-side up, and marked the design and did the quilting on the plain side. This total disregard for meshing the quilting pattern with that of the patchwork reflected their attitude toward patchwork. The patchwork had come into being as an economic necessity and its artistry and beauty were unappreciated. It was used for the lining, and it was assumed that it would never show.

Women who were especially adept at quilting, or who had time to devote to it, often supplemented the family income by taking in tops from neighbors who could not produce enough quilts for their own family's use. At the same time, there were professional designers - mostly tailors, dressmakers, or milliners - some of them men - who marked quilttops. Perhaps this began as a response to the demand of the middle class for the same design excitement the rich were importing from abroad. Or perhaps it was a natural outgrowth of the fact that the designing of the quilting is the most artistic and difficult part of the whole project, and the home worker may have felt the need of professional support. In any case, quilttops, particularly quilts for special occasions like weddings, could be "sent out" to be marked by a professional. Some professionals also sold marked quilttops in shops, or through itinerant peddlers, and the work of some of them, like John Gardiner and Elizabeth Sanderson in the 19th century, became so widely sought after that they had to take on apprentices to keep up with the demand. Their work was ornate, highly individual, and easily recognized. It was a highlight in a woman's life to own a Gardiner or a Sanderson, but it was a highlight because she and her friends were quilt markers themselves, and they could fully appreciate the artistry and professionalism that had gone into the marking of the top. Once they had finished quilting one of these prized tops, many women refused ever to wash the quilt, because they wanted the blue marking pencil - the trademark of the master-marker - to show permanently.

On this side of the water, the quilter was more on her own. Of course, the traditional patterns and techniques and the templates themselves came across the Atlantic with the English colonists, but the colonial quiltmaker, especially in the cold climate of Canada and New England, was under pressure to produce a fantastic number of quilts. She also had fewer materials to make quilts with than her English cousin, who lived in a great manufacturing nation. Unless she was wealthy enough to import fabric from England, she had to produce it herself, or salvage it from worn clothing or household goods. Because of these pressures, and because many of the colonists came from the north counties of England where, in contrast to the rest of England, patchwork was highly developed, the emphasis on this side of the Atlantic, both in the United States and in Canada, shifted to patchwork, and the art of quilting quickly regressed.

Utility quilts were often tied instead of being quilted because there simply wasn't time to quilt them. When utility quilts **were** quilted, fancy patterns were abandoned for quick and easy ones. Often an entire quilt would be done in a square or a hanging diamond, which could be quickly marked by two ladies on opposite ends of a chalked string. This method, sometimes called "pinging", is not highly recommended because its precision depends entirely on the true eye of the pingers, and often the lines aren't really parallel. But it was fast, and it got the job done, not only in colonial times, but out on the old frontier as well, where conditions were much the same.

Another, better thing that evolved out of this need to speed up the marking, was the custom of quilting parallel to the seam lines of the patching - about ¼" inside of each patch, by eye, without marking at all. In the United States, this is still the most common way of quilting a patchwork quilt, and it's often the best one. It's easy, and it's effective, because it repeats and re-enforces the artistic statement the patchwork is trying to make.

This is not to say that the art of fine quilting disappeared. There were many beautiful whole-cloth quilted counterpanes made in the colonies - in Linsey-woolsey, in linen, in cotton - which equalled, and eventually even surpassed, anything being done in England. Marking was done freehand or with templates, as it was in England. Some of the templates were made of cardboard; some of buckram; some of wood; some of tin. The tin ones look like cookie cutters, and probably a lot of museums are displaying them in the wrong department. Plates, teacups, and wineglasses were used as templates in the marking of curved patterns. Actually, anything you can draw around, even an oak leaf, can be a template.

In America as in England there were professional markers. Worse yet, there began to be professional quilters as well. Bit by bit, the homemaker became a patchworker who sent her top out to be professionally marked and quilted, not because she didn't have the time to do it, or the innate artistic ability to do it, but because she had convinced herself that marking and quilting were beyond her skills. The emergence of that attitude, which I think really peaked during the great quilt revival of the 1920's and 30's, is the worst thing that ever happened to American quiltmaking, and we are still trying to recover from it today.

Now, I'm not saying that there's anything wrong with you if you send your tops out to be quilted. Some of us like to patch; some like applique; some prefer to quilt. I'll admit that I think the designing and marking is the most fun. But most of us get the greatest joy of creation out of being able to do the entire project: salvaging the materials and figuring out how to make a thing of beauty out of them; piecing the top; designing and marking the quilting; quilting it and binding it and inviting our friends in so we can say, "Hey, see what I did!" Beginning and ending, and being able to know, "This is mine."

Commercialization of quiltmaking began early on this side of the Atlantic. Not only were there professional markers and quilters - and teachers, of course - but there were commercially printed patterns for both quilting and pieced work. And by pieced work I mean both patchwork and applique. This commercialization didn't do much damage to pieced work. After all, patterns were traditional and the quiltmaker needed a pattern. She might as well trace it out of a magazine or a pattern book as off her mother's template or her neighbor's quilt. The only thing it did was to tend to standardize the size of quilt blocks.

But the real harm in commercialization was done to quilting. Instead of marking either freehand or with templates, and fitting the design into the space, women bought stencils, which they could transfer to a quilt top with chalk or cornstarch, or they bought ready-drawn designs which they could transfer to the top by tracing or with carbon paper. **Then** the space had to be fitted into the design, often with poor results. In addition, the commercial pattern unit, repeated over and over without variation, gave an assembly-line appearance to the quilting. And, as if commercial patterns hadn't done enough damage already, they also took the **fun** out of pattern marking.

But now, at last, we are beginning to see creative quiltmakers trying to get their work away from professional designers and commercial producers, and to get it back into their own hands. We have come full circle, and the most modern among us are using the old techniques that came across the water with the first English settlers.

Marking a Meandering Vine

We have already discussed how to mark several favorite traditional quilting designs - the various feathers in Chapter II, the Cables in Chapter III - but I would like to add a word about the construction of the running or meandering vine. The vine, which to be effective, must take its leaves and often a blossom and/or a bud from the design of the quilt top, is called "running" if its curves are almost flat, and "meandering" if it loops along in a more sensuous manner. The vine in its applique form is often used as a border, but a quilted vine is no less effective as a means of restating the basic design of the quilt.

I chose a meandering rose and rosebud vine, backed with a close-set hanging diamond, for the Roses and Buds quilt in Plate XXII partly because it repeated the rose motif of the quilttop, and partly because it looked easy to design. First, I added it to a sketch of the applique design - drawing, erasing, drawing and erasing again, particularly at the corners, until I got a curve that satisfied me. Then I drafted a full-sized paper pattern of one-fourth of the quilt and worked out the design on that scale. A large French curve would have been perfect for drafting the curves, but I didn't have one. I therefore drew the curves free-hand and made cardboard templates of the ones leading into and out of the corner, so that they would be the same in all four corners of the quilt. I decided minor differences in other curved lines of the quilting pattern would cause no difficulty.

For templates, I used the cardboard template of the #1 rose and one made by combining the #5 calyx pattern with the #3 bud top. I then taped the quilttop to the ping-pong table to give me a firm surface for tracing, and using dressmaker's chalk (which I kept super-sharp with a pocket sharpener borrowed from my son) marked the entire surface, doing the meandering vine first and the background hanging diamonds last. Figure 44 gives a glimpse of the meandering vine in process as it went around one of the corners.

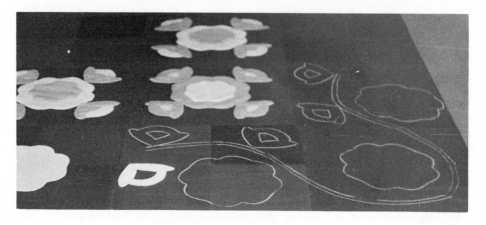

Figure 44 - Marking a Meandering Vine

Putting the Quilt in the Frame

Now that the quilting is marked on the top, and before it is partly erased by the admiring caresses of too many passers-by, it is time to put the quilt into the frame.

It's a big job to get a quilt into the frame, but if you were afraid of a big job you wouldn't be making a quilt. There are almost as many different ways to put in as there are quilters, and good craftswomen get good results in different ways. However, even though I consider my various results as a series of imperfections leading to the ultimate perfection, I do believe we should always use the method which is most likely to bring success.

Most quilters lay out their backing, their batting, and their top, and then tack all three to the rolling bars of the frame at once. This is easy, but it causes several problems. One is that you cannot quilt to the edge of the patchwork because of the tacks and because it is almost impossible to quilt right up to the bar. Another is that, particularly with a wool quilt backed with cotton flannel, each layer stretches differently, and so should be stretched separately.

Therefore, my first advice is to tack heavy muslin strips on to the rolling bars of your quilt frame so that you can **sew** your lining on rather than tacking it down. This will move it away from the bars so that you never have to quilt right up to them. If you make the lining larger than the top (two inches longer, and two wider is a good size), you will be able to quilt clear to the edge of the patchwork. Many quilters tack canvas on to the bars; some use a double thickness of unbleached muslin. Since using what is at hand is what quilting is all about, use whatever you have in your scrapbag - muslin, denim, duck, canvas. You should have at least an inch of material protruding beyond the bar when you've finished tacking it on.

Now, lay out your lining, right side to the floor between the two rolling bars of your frame. Sew the top and bottom of the quilt lining to the muslin strips along the rolling bars. Use a heavy cotton cord or a double thickness of heavy-duty thread.

Now, get a couple of one-by-ones, about eight feet long, at the lumber yard. You can usually persuade them to let you go through their scrap, and get these boards cheaply. If yours is a household where C-clamps are available, clamp a one-by-one under the rolling bar at one corner, in a position so that the lining will overlap the one-by-one by about ¼". If you don't have C-clamps, lash the two bars together with postal cord. Pulling it taut as you go, tack the lining to the one-by-one. Clamp the corner when you get to it. By measuring, clamp the remaining one-by-one into position, so that right and left sides are identical and then tack the lining to the second side.

If you pull the lining top too taut, it will stretch out of shape and snap back when released, making puckers in the quilt top. If you don't pull it taut enough, you might as well not have bothered with tacking it to the frame. So, like one of these recipes that says, "cook until done", I will tell you to stretch to the appropriate tautness, and you will have to accept that and experiment with it until you know how tight you like your linings.

Now, unroll your batting carefully so as not to tear it or pull it thin in places, and lay it on top of the lining. If you have great difficulty with this part of the process, switch to a better brand of batting next time. Some battings are absolutely impossible to work with, but there are many commercial battings available which unroll without difficulty.

Now, place the patchwork top, which has already been marked for quilting, right-side-up, on top of the other two layers. Again pulling it to the desired tautness, pin it to the lining all around the edges. Use straight pins if you are planning to baste before removing the quilt from this frame. Otherwise, use medium-sized safety pins. Now, start pinning from the middle of the quilt outward, telling yourself as you do so that all this bending and stretching is good for the figure. A pin per patch, or roughly a pin for every two square inches or so, is a good goal to strive toward. When finished, your quilt will resemble Figure 45.

If you are putting into a standard frame, pins work fine, and save a lot of time. You can then remove them as you work, and can count on them to hold the unworked portions in place until you get to them. If you are going to do machine quilting, or if you quilt in a large embroidery hoop, you will need to baste instead of pin. Start from the middle of the quilt, and run vertical, horizontal, and diagonal bastings all across the quilt, as well as all around the outside edges.

The two one-by-ones can now be removed, and the quilt can be rolled onto the bars. This is the moment when you realize why God put us into families, and gave us friends and neighbors. Rolling the quilt onto the bars is at least a two-woman job. Roll under, from top and bottom simultaneously, keeping the appropriate tautness, and roll straight. When you have rolled to the middle or almost so, insert the rolling bars into the frame and secure them there, adjusting the tautness of the material to your preference. If it is too taut, it will be hard to get small enough quilting stitches. Your quilt will also "snap back" and pucker when it is taken off the frame. A certain amount of this, however, is desirable, and if you haven't some tension on the material, you might as well have done the quilting in your lap, and not bothered with all this putting-in.

Most American quilters feel that the two rolling bars hold the quilt in place well enough, but the English quilters also pull the work out to the sides and secure it, once it is in the frame. This can only be done twelve inches at a time, of course, and is accomplished by pinning a strip of bias tape to the edge of the quilt next to the rolling bar. Run the tape out around the end of the frame, and pin it to the quilt again about two or three inches from the first pin. Continue lashing until all the exposed quilt has been pulled to the side. This is not much work, and gives a far firmer tension to the surface to be quilted.

The Technique of Quilting

Many modern craftswomen quilt one stitch at a time by the poke method, mostly because they have been unwilling to learn to quilt properly. Some get beautiful results this way; most do not. You should be able to get five or six stitches on your needle at once. Practice until you can, or each quilt will be a lifetime's project. If two stitches at a time is all you can handle now, start with two, but work toward three, then four, then five. Your finished work should exhibit small, even stitches, measuring somewhere between six and twelve to the inch.

Although it seems awkward at first, there is no way to be certain your stitches are catching all three layers without keeping your left hand under the work, at the point where the needle comes down through. Novices always have sore index fingers, but experienced quilters either develop callouses, or get smarter about feeling the needle and helping it along its way without getting pricked. If you have never quilted before, try to get someone to show you how she does it, realizing that this will be only a start. Each craftswoman has to work out her own methods for herself, but you don't have to start from absolute zero.

126

Figure 45 - Roses and Buds Pinned and Ready to Go into the Frame

Most American quilters quilt either from right to left, or from the center of the frame toward themselves. An English quilter, if you asked her in which direction she quilted, would give you a strange look and mutter something about quilting wherever the pattern went. Some of these English quilters solve the awkwardnesses of intricate pattern by quilting sometimes with their right hands and sometimes with their left. Certainly, it is easier to quilt right to left, or toward yourself, and I get better-looking stitches in those directions too. But sooner or later, unless you do strictly pedestrian designs, you are going to have to face up to going around corners in various directions.

CHAPTER 6

PRESSED QUILTS

The pressed quilt is so easy, so economical of materials, and so open to innovation, that it exerts a life-long fascination on many quiltmakers. A pressed quilt is any quilt in which, during its construction, the individual pattern pieces are consecutively sewed onto a foundation square, each one being pressed open after being stitched, to hide the seam line. The term "pressed quilt" is confusing, and pressed quilts are often called "string" quilts. String quilts are actually a special variety of pressed quilts, but all pressed quilts aren't string quilts. There is much inter-and overlapping of terminology, and an additional confusion arises because some quilts, like the Roman Square, the Pineapple, and Grandmother's Fan, are sometimes made as pressed quilts and sometimes as patchwork quilts.

For purposes of this chapter, at least, a pressed quilt is any quilt that is made by the pressed-work technique, and includes the Roman Square, the simple String Quilts, the Rainbows and Spider Webs, Log Cabins, and Pineapples.

The pressed-work technique is particularly well adapted to the making of wool quilts, because the foundation square compensates for the fabric's tendency to stretch out of shape, and most of the quilts that we have traditionally thought of as wool quilts are made by pressed-work techniques.

The Roman Square

Because the block (three rectangles sewed together into a square) was quickly and easily cut and stitched, and because it could utilize miscellaneous left-overs, the Roman Square was always a common utility quilt. It was often, if not usually, made of wool, and because of this fact, the pressed-work technique was more appropriate than the patchwork, and more often used. It was sometimes set in long strips, in which case it was called a Hit and Miss like its close relative of the same name, which was made with squares. Usually, however, the blocks were set so that the rectangular bands ran first horizontally and then vertically so that the block did not lose its integrity in the setting. This setting gives the over-all effect of web weaving, an effect which is sometimes accentuated by the use of light blocks vertically and dark blocks horizontally.

Often the block is made up of a light stripe set between two dark ones. Sometimes, the quiltmaker sorts her pieces into three piles, light, medium, and dark, and runs her shading across the square from light to dark. When the outside strip of the block is decidedly darker than the others, and the quilt is set so that these dark strips form a series of graduated stairs across the quilt as in Figure 46, the pattern is called Rail Fence.* Probably most of you have never seen an old-fashioned rail fence, but these beautiful old log fences zigzagging across the countryside were once a familiar aspect of the landscape.

Figure 46 - Roman Square, Rail Fence Set

*The Rail Fence usually has 4 strips, as in Figure 46.

The Roman Square can also be set diagonally, with the bands running from lower left to upper right in alternate rows, and from upper left to lower right in the others. If the setting triangles of a quilt set in this way are all the same color, they form an interesting self-border.

In the Victorian era, the Roman Square was made of exotic materials, and set with a latticework of black silk, which was in plentiful supply because every matron's "best" dress, which contained yards of material, was made of black silk. It is this Victorian version that usually comes to mind when the name Roman Square is mentioned, but the pattern is far more vigorous than that, and can be set in a great variety of ways. Nowadays, the Roman Square doesn't necessarily have only three or four rectangles to the block. Any square which is composed of rectangles is usually called a Roman Square.

Historically, whether through the desire to use ever-smaller scraps, or from the simple artistic impulse to push a design to the ultimate, these rectangular Roman blocks became narrow strips. Sally Garoutte of Mill Valley, California, found a tattered old wool Roman Stripe which her grandmother had made being used as padding in her father's workshop. Like many fine old pressed quilts, it was not tied, but quilted from the back, and the quilting was visible only from the reverse. Sally rescued the quilt, studied its construction, and made a contemporary copy out of heavy cotton materials. Her Roman block, which contains nine strips, is set in the standard way, with the strips running vertically in one block and horizontally in the next.

Sally's use of color is completely contemporary, and raises this old quilt pattern into the realm of textile art. The basic colors are blue, green, and brown. Starting in the upper left-hand corner with the lightest blues, Sally worked diagonally across the quilt, gradually darkening the blues and then working them into light greens at the lower right. The lower left corner is quite dark, and makes use of squares done in dark blues and brown, and in the medium-to-dark greens. The upper right corner contains some of the lighter blues, but it is basically made of medium and dark blue. Near the center of the quilt, but not in the exact center, is a horizontal block pieced with medium brown and bright red. A vertical blue block slightly below it and to the right, has **one** red stripe. These unexpected reds provide a focus and an interest to the quilt which a less secure artist would never have dared give it.

The success of Sally's quilt is proof that contemporary quiltmakers do not need to cut themselves off from the traditional patterns, techniques, and sets in order to make thoroughly modern quilts.

The string quilt, whether made from scraps put together at random, or carefully color-controlled by a textile artist, can be varied in an almost infinite number of ways without destroying the basic simplicity of its construction. For the string quilt is without doubt **the** simplest and fastest quilt to make. Although it can be made with patchwork methods, pressed-work methods are faster and more practical, and result in a quilt top that doesn't necessarily need an interlining, although some modern workers prefer an interlining, and sometimes even build one in, strip by strip.

How to Make a Pressed Quilt

All pressed quilts, from the simplest Roman Square to the most complicated Pineapple, are made by the same basic method. A background square, constructed from muslin or any woven fabric from the ragbag, is first cut in the same size the finished block will be, plus seam allowances. A 12-inch block, then, will be constructed on a 12½" backing.

Many pressed quilts are tied, but the finest examples are quilted, often invisibly. By that I mean that they are quilted from the back, catching the foundation fabric, but not the top, pressed layer. It is therefore a good idea to use a soft cotton for a backing, as the needle will go through it easily. I prefer old flannel from the ragbag for these backings - discarded pajamas, nighties, or boy's shirts - but other soft cottons do as well. Ragbag backings, in addition to their virtues in the economic line, add an element of nostalgia to the work. It's fun to work on backings cut from clothes you used to enjoy wearing, or from garments so small you can't quite remember that the children ever were that size.

Some of the more complicated pressed blocks, including the Log Cabin, start in the center of the square and work outward. Directions for putting them together are given later in this chapter. The simpler ones - the Roman Square, the Rainbow, and the block usually simply called String Quilt (as in Plate XXV), start from the edge of the square and work across, or from one corner and work diagonally.

To make the Roman Square block, first decide how you want your colors to progress. Then lay the first piece right-side up along the edge of the backing square, pin it in place, and stitch it to the backing, **outside** the seam allowance, i.e., about 1/8" from the edge of the square. Smooth it in place, and lay the second strip exactly on top of it, right sides together. Sew along the inside edge, through all three pieces of fabric, allowing a ¼" seam allowance. Press open, hiding the seam. Now you see why these quilts are called pressed quilts. Continue on, each time laying the new strip directly on top of the strip which has just been pressed open. Liberal use of pins, placed at right angles to the seam line, is highly recommended. When the last strip has been pressed open, again sew the outside edge down to the backing fabric, outside the seam allowance. If you leave these outside strips loose, they cause all sorts of trouble (of the puckering variety) when you start to set your blocks together. Hints on short-cuts and speed-up methods are given in the section on Log Cabins later in this chapter.

String Quilts

The String Quilt in Plate XXV was made by this same method by Emily Lucretia Forehand in the 1960's, when she was in her eighties. She made it during a seige in a nursing home in Fitzgerald, Georgia, when she was incapacitated by a broken hip. The quilt was made mostly from pieces of material cut off men's trousers while they were being shortened at the tailor's. It is backed with a red, green, and black polyester patchwork print. The multicolored feather-stitching done along the seam lines by her daughter, Clara Barton Turner, of Birmingham,

132

PLATE XXV
Contemporary String Quilt made by Emily Lucretia Forehand, Fitzgerald, Georgia, c. 1960. Note the interesting setting, which creates an optical illusion going back and forth between diamonds within diamonds and large X's. Note also the interest lent by the green satin blanket binding.

Courtesy Clara Elaine Rogers, Durango, Colorado

Alabama, adds greatly to the surface interest of the quilt.

Mrs. Forehand's block was made exactly like the Roman block just described, except that she started in one corner and worked diagonally across the backing square. It is not necessary to measure the strips in advance with this pattern (simply lay your strip in place; stitch it down; and then trim it even with the edge of the backing square), nor need the strips necessarily all be of the same width. Indeed, this particular quilt gets much of its interest from the fact that the widths of the strips vary.

Nothing could be easier than making a string quilt of this type, and it is highly recommended for beginners because of the assurance of success that it offers. The technique is simple and perfectly adapted to fast machine work. If wool is used rather than cotton, there is not even the problem of having to remember to put right sides together as the work progresses. Scraps of all sizes and colors can be used, and intuitional color planning as the work progresses is perfectly adequate.

A smooth, professional-looking surface does depend, however, on constant pressing, preferably with a steam iron. If it bothers you to keep jumping up and down and running from sewing machine to steam iron and back, work on several blocks at once. After a strip has been stitched and trimmed on each of several blocks, press all at the same time.

One of the points of this kind of a pattern is to use up random materials; however you should not be completely random when setting time comes. Lay your blocks out on the bed and arrange and re-arrange them until you get the effect you are after. Often a concentration of a given color - or of light or dark - at the center of the quilt will hold the pattern together visually, and a far more artistic quilt will result than if you had dispersed the colors evenly. Sometimes, if you have several shades of a given color, you can work out from the center of the quilt in that color, light to dark or even dark to light, and the rest of the blocks, even though they are miscellaneous in hue, will recede into the background. These suggestions are merely starting points; color sense is largely instinctive, and if you trust yourself and will take the time to shuffle your blocks around on the top of the bed, you will find many artistically satisfying color arrangements that no amount of theory could set out in advance.

An interesting string quilt results if each block is begun and ended with a triangle, if these triangles are kept exactly the same size and are cut from the same color in all the blocks. The wholly satisfying Victorian string quilt in Plate XXVI uses this pattern, combining velvet triangles with silk strips.

Needless to say, the size of the triangle used to begin and end the block will greatly affect the appearance of the finished quilt top, and you may want to experiment by quickly making blocks of four (which could later be used as pillow tops) with different-sized triangles before embarking on making an entire quilt top with this pattern.

Although string quilts are almost universally made with straight strips, this

134

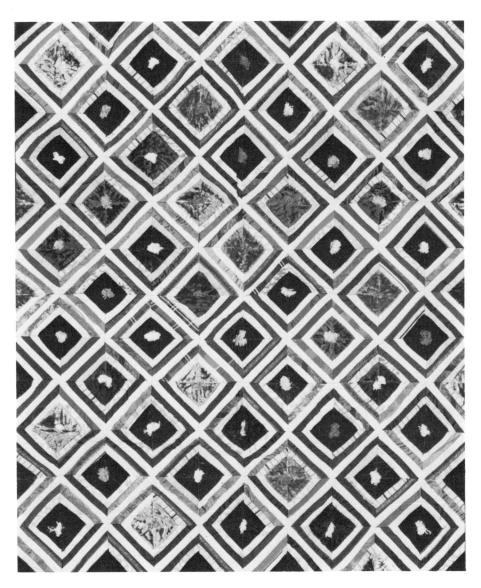

PLATE XXVI
Victorian String Quilt, silk and velvet. Although this quilt is light-weight and could easily have been quilted, its maker understood that greater design interest could be achieved by tying. See Plate XI for another example of a quilt enhanced by ties.

tradition is not necessarily binding on the expert. Michael James' Night Sky 2 is a consumate example of the possibilities of the string block when worked with curves. Each block is a string block begun and ended with a quarter-circle, and developed with curved pieces, mostly, but not exclusively, rainbow arcs. Exciting as the individual blocks are, Michael's real artistry is reflected in the setting together, where his balance between repetition and contrast produces an exciting whole.

The Rainbow Block

When you expand the size of the triangle and use it only once, you have a Rainbow block. A Rainbow block is a string block in which one-half the foundation square is covered by a single triangle, and the other half is covered with strips. To make your triangle pattern, simply fold the pattern for your foundation square in half diagonally. The Rainbow block makes a beautiful scrap quilt when set in blocks of four with the string halves of the blocks together, like the quilt in Plate XXVII. Note the additional surface interest provided by the simple quilting in the triangles.

I have seen Amish wool Rainbow quilts in which all the triangles were done in the same color, and the blocks then set in rows, with the string half of the block always to the upper right. This strong, vibrant pattern is then contained within a narrow border of one of the dominant colors, and the whole is enclosed in a wider border made from the same material as the triangles.

If the Rainbow block is pieced so that there is strong light vs. dark contrast between the two halves of the block, the squares can be set in any of the ways the Log Cabin square is set.

Spider Webs

Spider Webs (sometimes called Cobwebs) are simply string quilts constructed on pie-shaped foundations rather than on square foundations. Sometimes, the pattern for the pie-shaped piece is obtained by simply folding diagonally a square the size the finished block is to be. The triangle thus obtained is folded again, and then again, and one wedge is cut out along the fold lines. The more sophisticated spider webs, however, get their basic pattern from an octagon.

To draft this octagon, draw a line the length you want one side of the octagon to be on a piece of tracing paper. If you will think of the octagon block as squared-out, then draw this base line about one-third as long as the side of the square: i.e., 4" long for a 12" block, approximately. Using the angle given in Figure 47, measure an angle upward at each end of the base line and extend these new sides until they are **exactly** the same length as your base line. Continue on in the same way until you have an octagon. Check the accuracy of your drafting by folding the octagon in half to see if both halves are the same. Your finished product is only as good as your pattern, so keep trying until you get a perfect pattern.

PLATE XXVII
Detail, Rainbow Quilt, c. 1880, Pennsylvania.

Courtesy Rhea Goodman: Quilt Gallery, Inc., New York City

Figure 47 - Angle for Constructing an Octagon.

135°

Before you take out a wedge for your basic pattern piece, lay this octagon in the corner of a piece of typing paper, being certain that each side of the octagon is lying squarely against the edges of the typing paper, and mark off the triangle left in the corner. This is the pattern for your setting triangle, which you will use to square off the octagons before setting them into the quilt top. Remember to add a ¼" seam allowance on both the triangle and the wedge.

The individual blocks of the Spider Web are constructed exactly as they are for the simplest string quilt, except that the narrow end of the wedge is covered with a triangle instead of a strip. Draft your pattern for this triangle by simply drawing a line across the top of the pattern for the foundation wedge, ¼" farther down than you want the finished triangle to be. When piecing, always start with the triangle, pinning it down, and machine-basting it in place outside the seam line.

Except for the triangles, the color scheme for a successful Spider Web can be entirely unplanned, except for the fact that you should alternate your strips between light and dark, so that the "web" effect is not destroyed when the wedges are reassembled into an octagon. Needless to say, all eight wedges of a given block need to be the same, so it is perhaps wise to do one strip at a time on all eight, stop to clip and press, and then do another eight.

A museum-quality Spider Web quilt like the one on the cover, however, cannot be created without pre-planning the color. Note, for instance, the emphasis given to the web by the two double bands of black, and note also the sophisticated placement of the reds and pinks, both in the octagon and in the setting squares, which of course are made up of the setting triangles of the octagons, coming together when the squared-out octagons are set together. Although this is a scrap quilt, it is not an unplanned quilt, and could well serve as a model for all of your work with string quilts.

When you have constructed all your octagons, start on the setting triangles. They can be cut out of whole cloth, of course, and need not be pressed-work triangles. If you intend to use them as important pressed-work design elements as in the Pennsylvania quilt on the cover, however, you will have to plan their color carefully. Either mark where they are to be placed in the final setting, or set as you go, to make sure that the four triangles which were intended to make up a square together do in fact get set together.

Other String Quilts

Any basic pattern piece can be "strung", if I may invent a term, and we often see star patterns done with this technique. One particularly interesting Spider

Web, called Grandma's Star and Web, in which the central triangles of the basic pattern have been converted to diamonds (which form eight-point stars in the centers of the webs) is given in the November, 1977 **Quilter's Newsletter Magazine**, p. 26. In this quilt, the setting triangles also form pieced (rather than pressed) stars for a fabulously beautiful quilt top.

Log Cabin Quilts

The Log Cabin used to be thought of as a native American design, patterned after the ubiquitous log cabin of the ever-receding frontier. Its center, which was almost always red, was said to represent the chimney, and the light half of the block was assumed to represent the part of the house which was in the sunshine, while the dark half represented the part in the shadow. Home-grown moralists, however, thought of the light half as the sunshine of life, while the dark half represented the inevitable shadows. These sentimental interpretations undoubtedly contributed to the popularity of the quilt, which was made almost universally in North America from the 1850's onwards. It used to be assumed that the Log Cabin was an indigenous American pattern, but in fact it is almost certain now that the pattern came into the southern US from England. Jenny Shin, from Cheltenham, Gloucestershire, in England, the lecturer who accompanied the Bicentennial show, "British Quilts, 1820-1975" from England, said that the Barn Raising quilt pictured in Plate XXVIII was made in England by Mary Morgan (born Mary Thomas, in 1817) before she emigrated to Virginia in 1830 to keep house for two brothers who were coal miners there. Although we don't know, of course, that she brought the pattern with her, it is inconceivable that she did not. In any case, the quilt pictured here did not cross the water until 1976, and establishes the fact that the pattern was known in England at a date prior to any surviving American example.

As if that news were not enough of a blow to our New World chauvinism, Mary Conroy, a Canadian researcher, has discovered that the Log Cabin pattern was even known to the ancient Egyptians!*

The date of an individual Log Cabin quilt can best be ascertained by its fabric. The earliest American ones, made in the 1850's, were usually made of heavy wools. Later, cotton prints and wool challis became popular, and in the Victorian era - the 1870's and 1880's - exotic materials like velvet, silk, satin, and brocade were used. Contemporary workers, of course, draw from all three traditions, but it is not generally difficult to spot contemporary fabrics. You have to remember, though, when dating a quilt, that a fabric sometimes sits in the scrap bag even as long as a generation before being used, so quilts are always dated by the **newest** fabric included, unless it is obviously a part of a later repair job. Bindings, for instance, are replaced often, and are not a reliable means of dating a quilt.

How to Put the Log Cabin Block Together

The Log Cabin block, like the string quilts, is made of long narrow strips

---

*See the interesting photographs of cat mummies covered with log-cabin work on p. 56 of Conroy's **300 Years of Canada's Quilts**.

PLATE XXVIII
Log Cabin, Barn Raising Set, cotton. Made by Mary Morgan in England, before she came to the colonies in 1830.

applied to a foundation square by pressed-work methods. The block, divided diagonally between light-colored materials and dark-colored materials, depends for its effect on this contrast between light and dark, and in-between shades should be left for other projects. Any fabric or any combination of fabrics can be used in a pressed quilt, and the construction of a pressed quilt provides a wonderful opportunity to utilize difficult fabrics - mohair and heavy woolens; duck and other heavy cottons, such as velveteen and corduroy; and of course knits, which so many of us have in such unused abundance in the scrap bag.

When cutting log-cabin strips, first establish the true grain of the fabric either by tearing the first strip or by pulling a thread. If you are using remnants or recycled materials, you will have strips of varying lengths, of course. Use the shorter ones in the center of the block, where the distances to be covered aren't great, and the longer ones as you work outward. Don't ever throw away your tag ends. Piece them, using a diagonal seam as illustrated in Figure 48.

Having decided on the fabrics to use, it is a good idea to cut a good number of strips in advance. Here we can take a tip from braided-rug enthusiasts, who use a metal cutting guide that fits over the end of their scissors, and can be set to cut strips from ¼" to 1½" wide.*

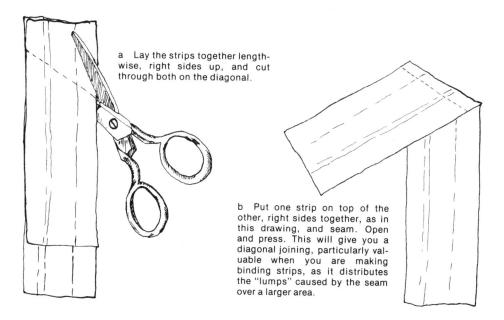

a   Lay the strips together length-wise, right sides up, and cut through both on the diagonal.

b   Put one strip on top of the other, right sides together, as in this drawing, and seam. Open and press. This will give you a diagonal joining, particularly valuable when you are making binding strips, as it distributes the "lumps" caused by the seam over a larger area.

Figure 48 - How to Piece Strips

Linda Shogren, the author of **The Log Cabin Compendium**, suggests a further efficiency. She cuts and pieces all her strips at once, and, rolling them up adhesive-tape fashion around a toilet-tissue core, puts them on a towel rod mounted behind her sewing machine so she can reel off each color as needed.

*I got mine from the Nu-flex Company, 246 First Ave. SO, St. Petersburg, FL 33701, for well under a dollar.

Complicated patterns are often given for Log Cabin blocks, but they are completely unnecessary. All that is needed is a square for the center and strips of material for the logs, as discussed above. The central square can be any size, and if you don't want to draft a pattern and cut squares in advance, you can cut your "square" material into strips, just as you do your "log" material, and get your square by folding the bottom of the strip up even with the side, as in Figure 49.

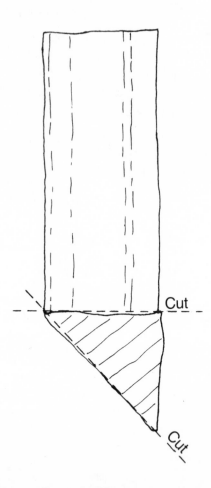

Cut

Cut

Figure 49 - No-pattern method of cutting squares and triangles. Cut a strip the width of the base line of your square or triangle. Fold the bottom of the strip up to the right-hand side of the strip and cut horizontally (on the dotted line) along the edge that used to be the bottom of the strip. This will give you a square. Get your triangle by cutting the square in half diagonally.

The logs themselves can be any width. Some quiltmakers pride themselves on using extremely narrow logs; others get a little edgy at the thought of cutting large pieces of material into tiny strips simply in order to sew them back together again. Needless to say, the appearance of the finished top is much affected by the size of the log, and you may want to experiment with several blocks before

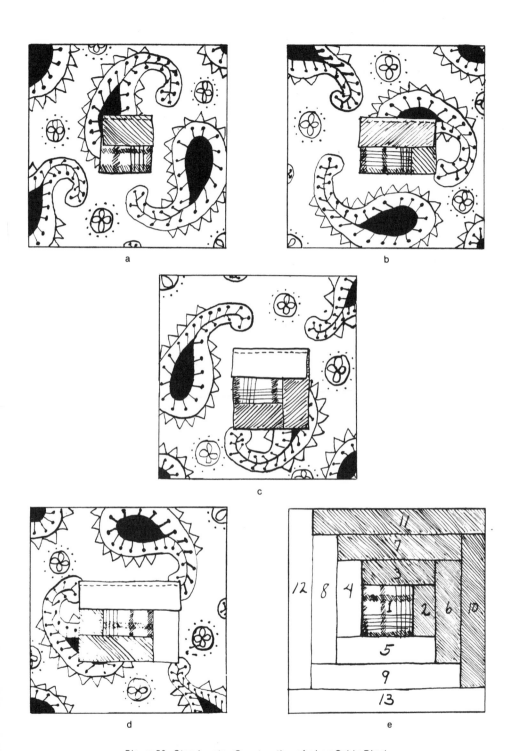

Figure 50 - Step-by-step Construction of a Log Cabin Block.

143

deciding on a strip width. Some contemporary workers are getting interesting effects by using strips of varying widths, but the traditional, invariably successful approach, is to decide on a log width and use it throughout.

Once all these preliminaries are over, you can sit down to your sewing machine and construct a large number of blocks quickly and efficiently. Since each strip has to be pressed before the next can be added, it makes sense to work on several blocks at once.

Place your square in the exact middle of the foundation square and pin it securely in place. Place a dark strip along the top of the square with the cut end flush with the upper left-hand side of the square right sides together, pin it in place, cut the strip even with the right-hand edge of the square, and stitch it down, allowing a ¼" seam allowance. Your work should look like Figure 50-a. Press the strip open, hiding the seam.

Turn your block clockwise, so that the strip you just added lies to the right of the square. Lay another dark log strip across the top of **both** the central square and the first log, pin, cut, and stitch. Your work should look like Figure 50b. Press open.

Again, turn your block clockwise, and, proceeding as before, add a **light** strip across the top, as in Figure 50c. Figure 50d shows the addition of the second light strip, which completes a square of logs around the central square.

Continue on, using Figure 50e as a guide, turning the block clockwise one turn between each addition, and remembering to add two dark logs, then two light logs, then two dark logs, etc., until the foundation block is covered.

Unless pure luck guided you, it will be apparent to you about the time that you are finishing up your first sample block, that **any** combination of central square, log width, and foundation square won't work. Decide on the sizes of your central square and your log first; then adjust the size of the foundation square to accommodate whatever number of logs you wish to build into each block.

Over the years, quiltmakers have evolved a number of different log-cabin squares, usually by varying the central square. Variations in the size of the central square are obvious. Sometimes, instead of a single square, three small squares, laid down side-by-side, are used. Sometimes a rectangle laid between two squares is used. We need not stop there, however. Any square, be it a yarn embroidery on wool or a patchwork rose, can be adapted as the center for a log-cabin block. Anne Orr's French Log Cabin, Plate XXIX, which was first published in the July 1931 **Good Housekeeping**, illustrates the effectiveness of elaborating the log cabin center. Anne Orr's patchwork center, which is composed of one-inch squares, is diagrammed in Figure 51.

Sets

There are many reasons for the enduring popularity of the Log Cabin quilt - its ease and speed of construction; its ability to utilize difficult materials, as well

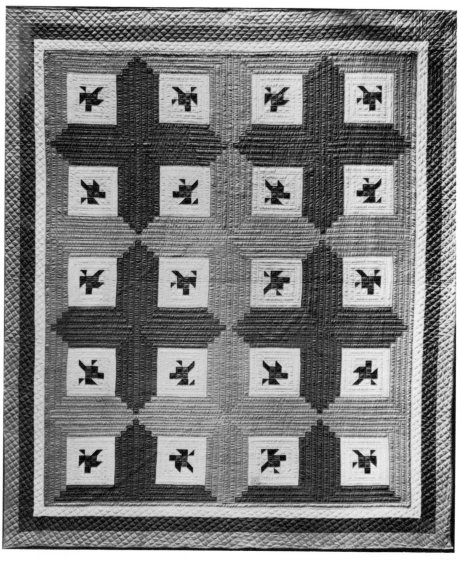

PLATE XXIX
Anne Orr's French Log Cabin, cotton, c. 1930. Note that the patchwork flowers are set at different angles in the different blocks.

Courtesy the Nashville Room, Public Library of Nashville and Davidson County, Nashville, Tennessee

as small, otherwise unusable scraps; and the pleasing results achieved with the pattern even by amateurs. I think an even more compelling reason for its popularity, however, is the opportunity it provides for personal expression by the almost unlimited variety of possible sets. The best-known sets have names of their own. When it is set, as in Plate XXVIII so that alternate light and dark concentric diamonds surround a central dark square (or vice versa) it is called Barn Raising, presumably because of the structural similarities to roof-trees. When it is set diagonally across the quilt in alternate light and dark steps, it is called Straight Furrow.* Set in alternate light and dark zigzags (Plate XXX) it is called Streak of Lightning; and the beautiful set in Plate XXXI is called Sunshine and Shadow. There is almost no end to the number of ways the light and dark halves of these blocks can be put together, and many make bold, modern statements. Before you decide on the setting you want to use for your Log Cabin, get ahold of Linda Shogren's **Log Cabin Compendium****, which pictures forty different ways in which Log Cabin blocks can be set together, each more exciting than the one before it. These sets, of course, can be used with any block which, like the Log Cabin block, is a square divided diagonally into a light half and a dark half.

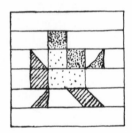

Figure 51 - Patchwork center for the French Log Cabin, 6" block. Each square equals one inch. Although the entire block can be pieced of one-inch squares, it is more efficient to cut rectangles when possible, and to piece in rows. Thus, the top and bottom rows are rectangles 1" x 6"; the next-to-the-top row is composed of a rectangle 1" x 2"; a 1" square; and a rectangle 1" x 3".

Color Control

Although the Log Cabin is usually a scrap quilt, it is not necessarily a miscellaneous or an unplanned quilt. Breath-taking results can be achieved if stringent color control is imposed. Holstein, for instance, in Plate 68, pictures a sophisticated color-controlled Barn Raising. All the lights are the same, but there are three darks (actually, two darks and a medium), the outside one repeating the red of the central square. This color scheme gives a unique appearance to the quilt, and illustrates once more the point that even though we all use the same patterns and even the same sets, we don't end up with the same quilts. In this case, the red, which is the outside dark strip of each block, forms a cross in the center of the quilt, and also forms zigzags between the white concentric

*If you're thinking of a Straight Furrow set, look first at the Straight Furrows on pages 66 and 67 of Bishop's **New Discoveries in American Quilts**, for a better treatment of corners than is usually achieved with this set.

**See Bibliography for details.

PLATE XXX
Log Cabin, Streak of Lightning Set, wool and silk, c. 1890 or earlier.

Courtesy Greenfield Village and the Henry Ford Museum, Dearborn, Michigan

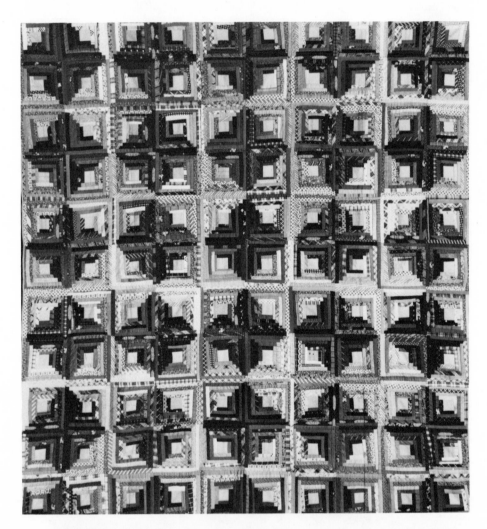

PLATE XXXI
Log Cabin, Sunshine and Shadow Set, c. 1850-90. Wool and silk, with wool turkey-red center squares. As in Plate XXX, the different reflective values of wool and silk were used here to create additional surface interest in this richly exciting quilt top.

Courtesy Greenfield Village and the Henry Ford Museum, Dearborn, Michigan

diamonds, providing a high degree of interest and cohesion to the quilt. Barn Raisings are not usually bordered (except among the Amish) but this one is, most successfully. If you are interested in experimenting with color control, by all means study this quilt while you are still in the planning stage.

Similarly, the Sunshine and Shadow Log Cabin is sometimes color-controlled for an entirely different effect from the traditional one. An early 20th-century Pennsylvania Sunshine and Shadow, pictured on page 65 of Bishop's **New Discoveries**, gets its heightened effect by working the dark halves of the blocks entirely in black, and by setting the outside light log of half the blocks in red, and the other half in green. When the blocks are set together, these red L-shaped pieces, set back to back, create an interesting design repeat. This red is picked up by the red centers, and the whole is bordered with a red and black sawtooth border somewhat inexpertly designed at the corners, but effective nonethelesss.

The straight Furrow and the Streak of Lightning patterns are often pieced with all the dark logs cut from the same color. This accentuates the set without giving up the desirable scrap-quilt qualities of the pattern.

If you opt for color control, you do **not** have to use all new materials. Several men's suits can be found in which the color - be it navy, black, gray, green, or brown - is close. An old blanket can provide ample material for the light logs. Don't overlook the possibilities of the dye pot. Rit dyes work fine with wools if you don't mind boiling them, and procion dyes, which are cold-water dyes, work well on wool too. Follow the directions carefully, however; dye only small amounts at a time to avoid a streaked end-result; and always **wash** the dyed materials some days afterwards to make sure that your fabrics are color-fast, before using them. Synthetics and synthetic blends do not take (or keep) dye well, and had best be left alone.*

Color control, then, gives bold statements and interesting effects, but it sacrifices the warm, homey glow of the unplanned country quilts. Be sure you know, before you start making the blocks, what it is you are trying to say with your quilt top.

Other Log Cabin Squares

When the Log Cabin square is pieced with the light logs in opposite, rather than adjacent, quarters, it produces a log cabin quilt called Courthouse Steps. A most unusual version, achieved by strong color control and self-bordered by the same method, is pictured on p. 126 of Bishop and Safford's **America's Quilts and Coverlets**.

Pineapples

The pineapple, which was a symbol of hospitality, was widely used in colonial American decoration, and there are a number of quilt patterns called pineapples. In the Log Cabin family, a pineapple is a Log Cabin square, usually with an embellished center, in which the laid-on pieces radiate outward from the corners of the central square as well as from their midpoints.

*If you don't know whether or not a fabric is synthetic, set a match to a small piece of it. Synthetics don't burn, they dissolve, forming small balls along the dissolving edge. Wool can be identified, when burning, by its familiar smell, and by the fact that it leaves nothing but ash behind.

Pineapple Variation

Most pineapples are made with ever-lengthening trapezoids working out from the center, but a simpler variation of the pattern, shown in Figure 52a, has trapezoids working out from the midpoints of the central square, and triangles radiating out from its corners.

To make a practice square like the one in Figure 52a, draft a 12" flannel square and a 3" black wool square. Fold both in half diagonally and press. Unfold, and fold again diagonally in the other direction, pressing again. You now have an X which will give you the exact center of each square. Place the exact center of the 3" square on the exact center of the 12" square, with the diagonal lines of the black wool on top of the diagonal lines of the flannel. Pin in place.

Draft a triangle with a base line the length of the side of the central square (in this case, 3"), and cut four of these triangles from plaid wool. Use them to square out the central black square, as in Figure 52b. You have now completed your elaborated center. Some pressed-work pineapples have pieced-work centers, and you may find it easier to piece your centers all at once before beginning the pressed work.

An easy way to cut these triangles without a pattern is to cut a straight strip 3" wide. Turn the lower left-hand corner of the strip up to the right-hand edge as in Figure 49, and cut along the upper edge of the triangle so formed, to get a square. Then cut along the diagonal to get two triangles.

Cut a 1¼" strip of grey worsted and attach a strip to each side, log-cabin fashion, as illustrated in Figure 52d-h. Press open.

Add a second series of plaid triangles, as in Figure 52j, pinning in place carefully so that the seam line barely touches the apex of the triangle, and does not flatten it into a trapezoid. Pressed open, your block will now look like Figure 52k, which shows the order of attachment.

You can now proceed to make the block any size you want to, alternating rows of gray strips with rows of plaid triangles. Since this is an all-over pattern, you can get a more interesting surface design, when it goes together, by substituting a black triangle for the plaid one on the final round. These triangles will set together into squares, echoing the black central squares.

The Basic Pineapple

The basic pineapple is usually called Windmill Blades, because of the feeling of motion generated by the ever-lengthening trapezoids radiating outward from the corners and the midpoints of an embellished center. As with the Log Cabin, the center is traditionally red, but this is not an invariable rule. That tradition was followed, however, in the Scottish quilt pictured in Plate XXXII, and both these centers and the square diamonds formed when the quilt was set together are also quilted in red thread. This is the only place on the top where the reverse quilting shows.

a   block diagram

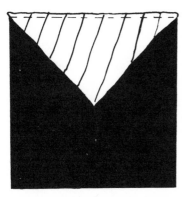

b   construction of elaborated center

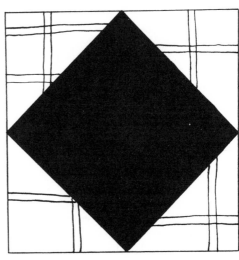

c   elaborated center

Figure 52 - Pineapple Variation

151

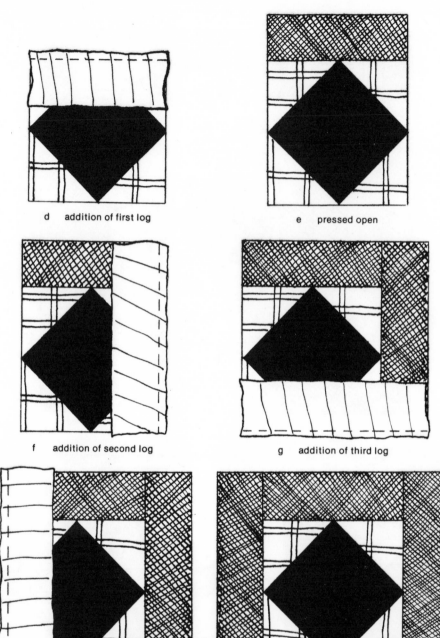

d   addition of first log

e   pressed open

f   addition of second log

g   addition of third log

h   addition of fourth log

i   appearance of block after the
first four logs have been added.

Figure 52
continued

j   addition of first row of triangles

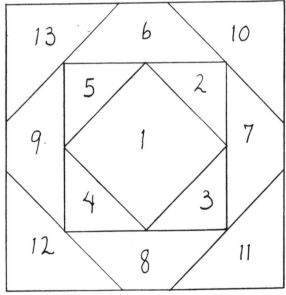

k   diagram of Pineapple Variation, showing the
order in which the pieces are added.

Figure 52
continued

Windmill Blades is a difficult quilt to make. Just as a log cabin would soon start to sag and settle if the corners were not true, so your Windmill Blades will not turn in the wind if your construction is not absolutely perfect. Not only does each row of strips have to be applied exactly parallel to the row before, so that the blades themselves are symmetrical, but the blades of each block have to be in the same place on the block so that when the quilt is assembled the blades join to form windmills in the foreground and stars in the background. You will note that the failure of the blade to join perfectly is a discordant note in one block of Plate XXXII.

Because of these difficulties, pieced-work techniques are often used instead of pressed-work techniques when working with this pattern, but pressed-work techniques are preferable when working with wool because of the support the backing square gives to the construction. It borders on the impossible, however, to get a first-class job with this pattern by using strip methods, so I have given you pattern pieces in Figure 53abc for a 12-inch block.

For each block, cut:

1 12½" flannel backing square
1 #1 square, red
4 #2 triangles, dark
4 each, #4, #6, #8, #10, #12, #14 trapezoids, light
4 each, #5, #7, #9, #11, #13, #15 trapezoids, dark
4 #3 triangles, red

Needless to say, the darks and the lights can be reversed. The thing to remember is to keep the even-numbered trapezoids one way and the odd-numbered ones the other way.

Construct the block exactly as you would any other Log Cabin: start with an elaborated center, made with the #1 square and the #2 triangles; then add the trapezoids, by ascending number, the dark ones at the corners of the elaborated center; the light ones at the midpoints.

Specifically, pin the #1 square in the exact center of the backing square. Add a #2 triangle to each side, right sides together. Pin and stitch, allowing a ¼" seam allowance. Press open. You will again have a square.

Add a #4 trapezoid to each side; press open. You will now have an octagon. From now on, continue adding trapezoids in numerical order, but since we only have four of each, and we are working with an eight-sided block, we will add only to every other side. This sounds confusing, but it isn't, because we simply add dark trapezoids to dark and light to light as we work outward.

When the #15 trapezoid has been added, square out the octagon by adding the four #3 triangles. These are usually cut from the same color the #1 square was, so when the quilt goes together they make square diamonds which seem to surround the central square in an interesting way, as in Plate XXXII.

154

PLATE XXXII
Detail, Scottish Woolen Pineapple Quilt, made in Hawick in 1880, first shown in the
United States during the Bicentennial British Exhibition, "British Quilts 1820-1975".
The materials in this quilt are particularly interesting, as its 3/8"-wide trapezoids
include many Scottish tartans.

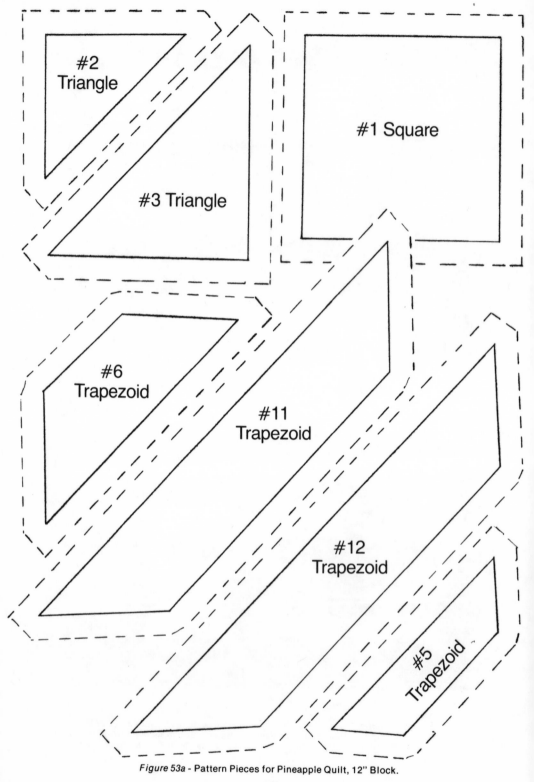

Figure 53a - Pattern Pieces for Pineapple Quilt, 12" Block.

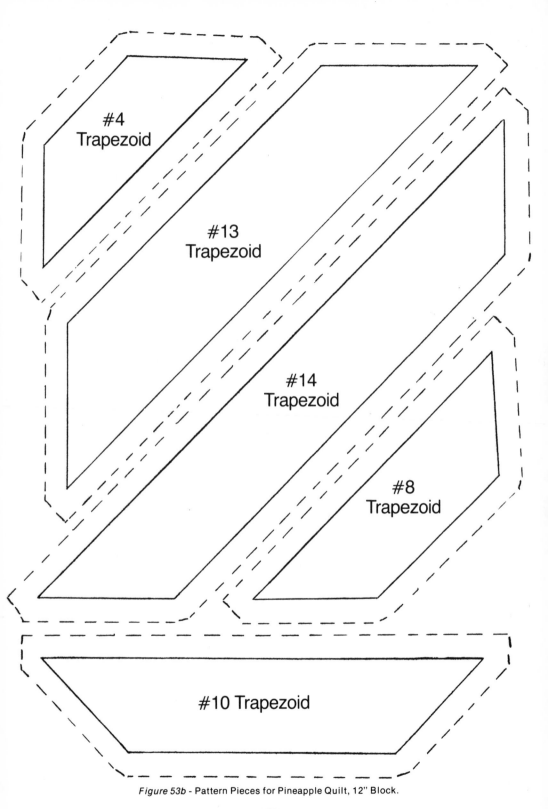

Figure 53b - Pattern Pieces for Pineapple Quilt, 12" Block.

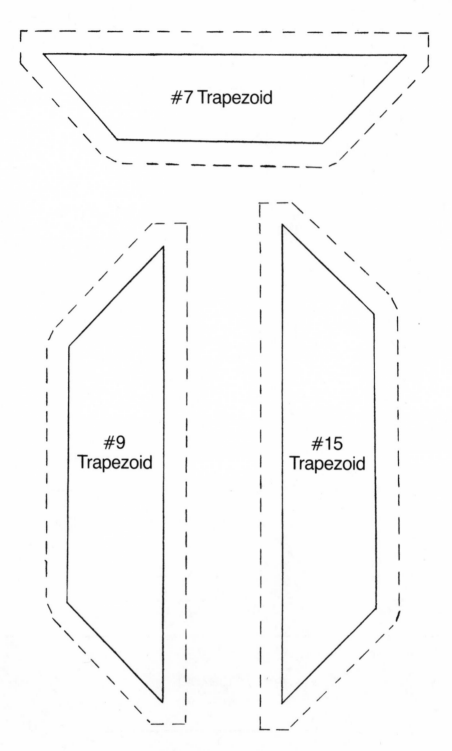

Figure 53c - Pattern Pieces for Pineapple Quilt, 12" Block.

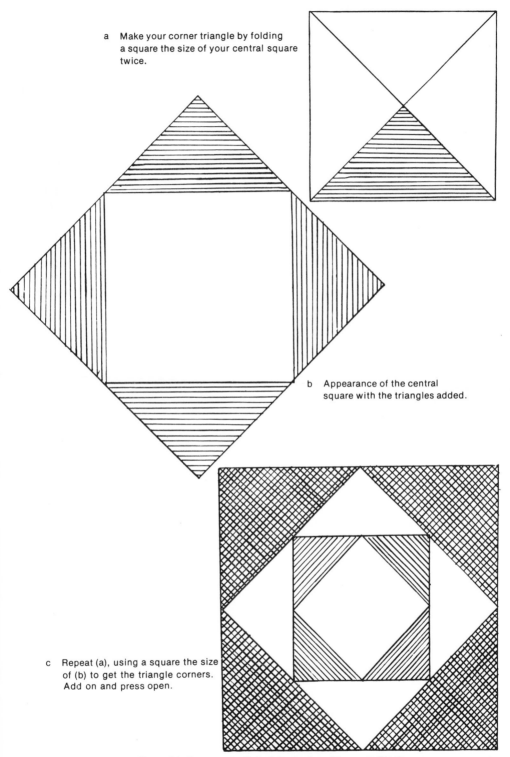

a Make your corner triangle by folding a square the size of your central square twice.

b Appearance of the central square with the triangles added.

c Repeat (a), using a square the size of (b) to get the triangle corners. Add on and press open.

Figure 54 - Super-embellished Center for a Pineapple Block.

159

When constructing an entire quilt top, this is an awfully lot of trapezoids to keep track of. You might want to cut and construct all the centers first; then cut and add all the #4 trapezoids; then all the #5 trapezoids, etc., so that your entire house will not be cluttered up with little piles of different-sized trapezoids.

Color Control in the Pineapple Pattern

Although the pineapple quilts are usually scrap quilts, they are often given greater coherence by severe color control. I don't mean that the quiltmaker went out and bought yards of new material; far from it. But she saved her reds, greens, blacks, whatever she wanted to use, until she had enough to make the entire top from them. Bishop's **New Discoveries** pictures one such (Plate 91) in which the light trapezoids alternate between red and gray; and the dark between black and maroon. This quilt is unusual because it is put together with narrow lattice strips. They slow down the motion of the quilt considerably (as do the four narrow borders). You might find this a good device to use if your pressed work turns out to be not quite perfect, as it would minimize or even hide any failure of the windmill blades to come together perfectly. Be careful to keep the lattice narrow, however, so that the motion of the blades is not stopped completely.

Another interesting example of color control in the pineapple is pictured in Plate 59 of Holstein's book. Here a super-embellished center (as in Figure 54) done in red, gold and white assumes a great importance. The strips of the dark blades alternate between red and green; while the light ones alternate between white and pink prints.

The pineapple is a difficult quilt to make, both from the point of view of construction and of color planning. It is more prone to disaster on both fronts than most patterns, and is not recommended for a beginner. However, with a little color control, or top-notch intuitive color choice (which most of you have, if you will trust it), this can be a beautiful quilt. You need to decide in advance, however, about the size and elaboration of the central "square" of the block; about the width and number of trapezoids per block; about the size of the block itself. All these decisions, of course, will have to be made on the basis of the material you have on hand; the size of your bed; the decor of the room; and your general ability as a pineapplist.

Hexagonal Logs

The pressed hexagon, an easy and effective variation of the Log Cabin square, is sometimes called Church Steps. To make a sample block, draft the pattern for the cotton backing as follows: draw a 6½-inch line on a piece of tracing paper. Using the angle given in Figure 30, Chapter IV, measure a 120° angle upward at each end of the base line, and extend these new sides to 6½ inches. Connect the two new sides, and you have half a hexagon. Pin the long side of this half-hexagon on the crosswise fold when cutting.

Now, cut your wool strips into 1½-inch widths, using a rug strip cutter for speed and convenience as described earlier in the chapter. Half your strips should be of a light-colored material, and half dark, and you should strive for contrast in

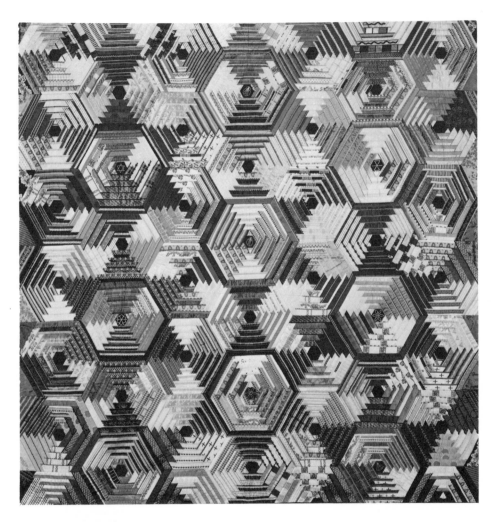

PLATE XXXIII
Log Cabin Quilt, Hexagon Variation, silk, made by Miss Jane Tucker, assisted by her niece, Miss Angie Tucker of West Gardiner, Maine, 1890. Note the embroidery motifs on some of the small center hexagons.

Courtesy Philadelphia Museum of Art: given by Miss Harriet Plimpton

texture as well as in color. A soft tweed or a fleecy surface in one material, for instance, will be set off by the smooth, tight surface of a worsted suit. Hard-to-use materials such as brocade, silk, knits, and velveteens can be used with this pressed quilt technique, if they are appropriate to the use the quilt will get. The Philadelphia Museum of Art quilt in Plate XXXIII is made entirely of silk, probably to be used as a throw over the back of a Victorian couch. Many Log Cabin quilts, designed to be used as bedspreads, or counterpanes as they used to be called, combine wool and silk or velvet with great effectiveness.

To proceed with our sample block, cut a plain wool hexagon from the pattern in Figure 30, Chapter IV, and fold it in half, both vertically and horizontally, pressing both folds in with the steam iron. Do the same with the large cotton hexagon. This will enable you to pinpoint the exact center of each hexagon so that you can get the small one exactly in the middle of the large one.

Now, pin dark strips to every other side of this small wool hexagon, cutting each strip to conform to the side of the hexagon, as in Figure 55abc. Sew, and, using a steam iron, press back away from the center of the block. Sew light strips to the three remaining sides, extending the light strips to cover the dark strip at each end, as in Figure 55b.

Continue adding dark and light alternately, pressing as you go so that each strip can overlap the ends of the one before it as in Figure 55c. After the final pressing (when you reach the edge of the cotton hexagon), turn the block over and trim the wool to conform to the size and shape of the cotton backing.

This sample hexagon will take five rounds of each material. Any size hexagon can be used, of course, and the strips can be cut into any width.

Many interesting settings can be used with hexagons. The quilt pictured in Plate XXXIII is set together as an all-over pattern, and produces an interesting optical quilt that moves among stars, circles, hexagons, and windmill blades. Hexagons can also be set with diamonds, with triangles, or with stars, as in the Evening Star quilt (Plate XVIII) discussed in Chapter IV.

Grandmother's Fan

Many Victorian Grandmother's Fan quilts were made from a richly varied collection of wools, silks, satins, brocades, and velvets which did not lend themselves readily to patchwork, and they were generally made by pressed-work methods. Like crazy quilts, they were sometimes used as expressions of the feminine desire for the super-ornate, in which case they were embroidered along the structural lines in a variety of fancy patterns. Sometimes, instead of embroidering along the structural lines, the quiltmaker utilized the surface provided by the #2 quarter circles and the #3 background. A dazzling wool and cotton fans quilt of this type is pictured in Plate 96 of Orlofsky's book. This quilt also has an interesting embroidered border.

The long curved seam of the fan pattern, which is impossible to deal with by pressed-work methods, was usually top-stitched without turning under the seam

a

b

c

Figure 55 - Construction of a Log Cabin Hexagon

163

allowance, and covered with fancy braid. Like other pressed quilts, the pressed Grandmother's Fan was usually tied rather than quilted.

To make a Grandmother's Fan block, use the pattern given in Figure 33, Chapter IV. Cut 7 #1 spokes, 1 #2 quarter-circle, and 1 #3 background. Although this is definitely a scrap quilt, many Victorians gave it unity by using the bright colors in the spokes, the dark colors in the #2 quarter-circles, and neutral colors in the #3 backgrounds. It's not a bad rule of thumb, and some sort of organization is necessary to prevent a completely miscellaneous surface. There are many Victorian fans in which all the #2 pieces are cut from the same material, all the #3 backgrounds from another material, and only the #1 spokes are cut from miscellaneous scraps. Needless to say, the fan spokes provide a wonderful use for discarded men's ties, particularly if the #2 and #3 pieces are cut from wool, which has much more subdued reflective qualities.

To assemble the fan block:

1. Lay out your seven spokes into a fan on the table top with the colors arranged as you want them to be in the finished block.

2. Cut a 10" square from muslin or other backing material and mark off the #2 quarter circle in one corner.

3. Sew the outside #1 spoke along the edge of the square, making sure that the seam allowance of the narrow end of the spoke is within the marked-off quarter-circle.

4. Lay the second #1 spoke on top of the first, right sides together, pin, and seam through all three layers (the backing square, and both spokes). Fold open and press.

5. Lay out the third spoke on top of the second, right sides together, seam and press. Repeat until all the spokes are in place.

6. Make a cardboard template of the #2 quarter-circle **without** the seam allowance, put it on top of the #2 wool quarter-circle, and press the seam allowance of the **curved portion only** back on top of the cardboard template. If the wool won't hold a curve, baste. Most wool pieces have enough stretch that this can be accomplished without clipping along the curve. However, if you are using brocade or silk or velvet, you will have to remove a notch or two from the seam allowance at the steepest points along the curve.

7. Place the pressed #2 quarter-circle in the corner, making sure that it covers the exposed ends of the spokes. Top-stitch or blind-stitch in place.

8. Pin the #3 background into place, without trying to turn under the seam allowance, and cover it with braid. Stitch into place.

Before you decide on the setting for this quilt, read the section of Grandmother's Fans in Chapter IV, and look at some of the common settings illustrated in Figure 34.

We have seen, then, that we have in the pressed-work technique the means to use any material - however intransigent - in quiltmaking. Pressed-work quilts, from the simple string to the difficult pineapple, adapt themselves well to machine work, and there is, in every family of quilts discussed in this chapter, unlimited opportunity for originality and innovation.

c

PLATE XXXIVabc
Embroidered Details from one of a pair of Crazy Quilts made by Sarah Dickinson, Wisconsin, c. 1870.

Courtesy Barbara Todd, Durango, Colorado

CHAPTER 7

CRAZY QUILTS

A crazy quilt is a collage in cloth. It is worked, like the pressed quilts, on a foundation block, but usually applique, rather than pressed-work, methods are used.

Although crazy quilts were not an exclusively Victorian manifestation, it is the lavish Victorian examples that have survived, both in memory and in fact. They were a parlor item, made, at an extravagant expenditure of time and energy, not (usually) for bedcovers, but for display. They were made from rich and exotic materials, and are characterized by extraordinary surface embellishment. As a rule, every seam line was covered with embroidery. Sometimes a feather stitch was used throughout, to give unity to the whole, but more often the surface was viewed as a vehicle for exhibiting the artist's fine embroidery technique, and many stitches were used. Dorothy Bond has studied hundreds of these Victorian quilts and preserved their stitches in her book, **Embroidery Stitches from Old American Quilts***. If you want to make a Victorian-type Crazy Quilt, her book is an obvious must.

Often, "plain" blocks were decorated with hand-painted designs; with commercial satin-stitch embroideries (florals like the one in Plate XXXIVa were most common, but I have seen a number of Victorian quilts which displayed an elegant commercial peacock); and with whimsical designs done in outline stitch, like the ones in Plate XXXIVb & c. Many of these were taken from the Kate Greenaway story books so popular at the time, but there were undoubtedly other commercial transfer designs available as well. Walt Disney characters, or illustrations from Winnie The Pooh, or the Mary Poppins books would be appropriate on a contemporary crazy.

Many persons consider a crazy quilt the very excrescence of Victorian taste, and I'm sure we've all seen many which are. Yet, at the Denver Art Museum show in 1974, where there were dazzling displays of both patchwork and applique, it was the crazies that were attracting the most attention. Many viewers, especially middle-aged male viewers, stood rapt in front of the crazy quilts, saying, "We had one of **those** at home", or, "**My** mother made one of those".

The crazy quilt, then, has a sentimental pull, and it's back in vogue again - both in its Victorian form and in a contemporary form - because it's **fun** to work with. Like the pressed quilt, the crazy can accommodate difficult materials, as well as small, otherwise unusable scraps. For many women, putting a cloth

*See Bibliography for details.

167

PLATE XXXV
Crazy Quilt with appliqued olive-green inner border made by Alpha Michener, Toronto, Ontario, Canada between 1890 and 1895.

Courtesy of the Royal Ontario Museum, Toronto, Canada

collage together in a balanced and satisfying way seems more creative than setting geometric blocks. While embroidery is usually used on the Victorian crazy quilts, that was a Victorian expression, not a crazy expression. Many crazies have no embroidery, and depend for their effect on interest of color and line. When big pieces are carefully color controlled, the crazy quilt is capable of making a stark contemporary statement, in perfect harmony with the most modern decor.

Although the crazy is usually not interlined, some contemporary workers are charmed by the puffy look, and have developed efficient methods for inserting an interlining as the work progresses. Dixie Haywood's book has a good discussion of these modern machine methods.*

The technique of the crazy quilt is not difficult. Cut a piece of unbleached muslin or other woven cotton to the size you have decided to work with, whether it be the size of the finished quilt, of a section, or of a single block. If you are making crazy-clothing, cut your section the shape of the pattern piece, but ¼" larger (½" larger if you plan to interline) to accommodate the inevitable taking-up that occurs.

Starting in the lower right-hand corner of the muslin, tack down the piece of fabric you have decided to use in that corner. Overlap the next piece, turning the edges under. Proceed, according to pre-determined plan or by experimentation, remembering to vary color, texture, and line, and remembering to save some of each fabric for use elsewhere in the quilt. You will find that the heavier materials - ribbon, brocade, velveteen - are more easily tucked under other fabrics, while the lighter-weight ones are easy to turn under and generally go on top. While some crazies are made entirely with straight lines (as for instance the quilt in Plate XXXV), the eye delights in contrast (**and** in curves), and your finished result will be more pleasing if you employ them at least to some extent. Wools and silks are particularly useful in the creation of curved lines, while the stiffer materials are used for straight-line effects. Remember, too, not to lose your overall balance in the quest for richness of texture and variety of line.

Pin or baste each piece in place, and then cover the structural lines with embroidery. Some quilts are unified by the use of a single color of embroidery floss throughout. Most, because the quilt is created partly to utilize what is on hand in scrapbag and workbasket, use many colors, textures, and thicknesses. The thickness, of course, can be controlled by the number of strands of floss simultaneously threaded through the needle.

If you are making a modern crazy, and will have no embroidery, blind-stitch the pieces in place, or (if you prefer machine work) top-stitch them. The choice between hand work and machine work will probably depend here on the fabric and the use the quilt will get. Exotic fabrics probably deserve hand work; heavy woolens and cottons for a utility quilt which will see hard wear and frequent washing are more appropriately done by machine. Don't be convinced that there is no precedent for machine top-stitching on crazy quilts. I have a box of oblong wool crazypatches put together about 1915 with machine top-stitching.

*Haywood, Dixie, **The Contemporary Crazy Quilt Project Book**, Chapter II.

To work successfully in the crazy format, you have to give it either space or organization if it is not to deteriorate into utter chaos. The easiest way to give crazy-work space - think of it as breathing room, if you like - is by latticework. Wool crazy blocks, set either square or diagonally, are often put together with black velveteen lattice strips, but some of the "fancier" lattice sets are even more appropriate to crazywork. Consider a zigzag, if your blocks are square, or give some thought, while you are still in the planning stage, to a more exotic block shape - a rectangle, a long hexagon, an octagon - which by its very shape demands a more interesting set. Even a square set with a square lattice can be elaborated, as illustrated by the Pennsylvania quilt (c. 1870) pictured in Plate 79 of Holstein's book. Here the cotton crazy blocks are set with a receding print which has a more calming effect than a stark, plain color would. Squares set at the intersections of the lattice work are of a similar print, in a darker tone of the same color. Is this slightly more elaborate lattice more appropriate to the crazy work than a plain lattice?

Another quilt, made by the same woman and pictured in Plate 80, squares out the crazy block with triangles before they are set into the lattice work, and that's a workable thought to keep in the back of your mind.

We occasionally see crazy blocks set alternately with plain blocks, and this is particularly effective in wool, where the fabric itself has such a glowing surface. Borders, too, provide a strong control, and Alpha Michener's crazy quilt (Plate XXXV) illustrates how an inner border, in particular, quiets the surface. This particular quilt was made all of a piece (a formidable undertaking) and the border was appliqued onto the surface, but a similar quilt could be planned in which the outer strips were constructed separately. From the point of view of technique, this would be easier because it would involve working with smaller pieces.

Pushing this border idea even farther, you might want to give some thought to the use of crazy work in other kinds of framed medallion quilts. Some of the quilt formats given in Figures 12, 13, and 14, Chapter III, might lend themselves well to crazy work

I think it might be a good idea to stop for a moment here to consider the importance of this single inner border in Alpha Michener's quilt, illustrated in Plate XXXV. Try to picture to yourself how this quilt would look without it. The quilt, although it has variety of color and texture, has no curved lines; all the pieces are approximately the same size; and it has no focus or attempt at organization. Without the inner border, it could easily have competed for the title of the most uninteresting crazy quilt ever made. But by this one stroke of genius - the addition of the simple inner border - this quilt became an unqualified artistic triumph. Think about that when you think about crazy work.

Crazywork is sometimes used as an element of organized patchwork. Sometimes the diamonds of a LeMoyne star, for instance, will be cut from crazywork, and the star spokes of the Rocky Road to Kansas are invariably cut

PLATE XXXVI
Wool Crazy-fan Quilt made by Susan McCord, Indiana, c. 1880.

Collection of Greenfield Village and the Henry Ford Museum, Dearborn, Michigan

from crazywork.* Crazywork can be controlled without being patterned, however. In the Victorian era it was frequently combined with the Grandmother's Fan. The fan is a bold enough pattern to stand up to the crazywork, and of course both patterns saw their greatest popularity during the same era. Sometimes fans were set into the four corners of a crazy quilt, sometimes four fan blocks were set together to form a wagon wheel in the center of an otherwise unstructured crazy quilt.

Susan McCord's wool crazy-fan (Plate XXXVI), made about 1880, however, is the finest example of the use of the fan with crazywork I know of. Susan McCord managed to control crazywork with the fan without patterning it, and in so doing raised crazywork to the status of textile art. Note that in this quilt, each block is different. Most have a fan in each corner, but some blocks have only two or three fans. The fans, of course, were not cut from patterns, but are free-wheeling and utterly unique.

Study the individual blocks of this quilt. Each can stand alone, as an interesting textile design in its own right, and each, I am sure, was constructed without thought to the others **except** in regard to color and texture. But you can be sure that the quilt was not set together in a miscellaneous manner, but was laid out on floor or bed where the squares could be combined and recombined until they formed a whole that satisfied its maker. This quilt has the same primitive, we might almost say accidental (if we didn't know better) charm that the string quilt in Plate XXV, Chapter VI, has. Organization and artistic effectiveness have been achieved in both without resorting to strict pre-planned structure, and the appeal of the approach involved in both these quilts is considerable to the quiltmaker whose talents lie more in the artistic than in the technical area.

*Dubois, Jean, **A Galaxy of Stars: America's Favorite Quilts**, see p. 66 ff for directions, patterns, and photos of successful Rocky Road to Kansas quilts.

CHAPTER 8

CONCLUSION

We have seen, then, in this leisurely ramble together, that the wool quilt is capable of doing anything that the cotton quilt can do, either alone or in combination with other fabrics. We have considered wool's economic advantages in quiltmaking - its warmth, its availability in recycled form. We have felt the emotional pull of its glowing colors. We have fallen under its spell.

We have gone over special techniques, particularly pressed-work techniques, designed to overcome the difficulties involved in working with wool. We have traversed the history of the wool quilt and immersed ourselves in its tradition in order, not only to enjoy it for its own sake, but to enable ourselves to build on it in an attempt to transcend it in our own, contemporary, work.

We are ready now to be artists in wool ourselves.

BIBLIOGRAPHY

Bassett, Margaret Byrd, **Profiles and Portraits of American Presidents and Their Wives**, Bond Wheelwright Co., Freeport, Maine, 1969.

Bishop, Robert, **New Discoveries in American Quilts**, E.P. Dutton & Co., Inc., New York, 1975.

Bishop, Robert and Elizabeth Safanda, **A Gallery of Amish Quilts: Design Diversity from a Plain People**, E.P. Dutton & Co., Inc., New York, 1976.

Bond, Dorothy, **Embroidery Stitches from Old American Quilts**, 1977, available from 34706 Row River Rd., Cottage Grove, Oregon 97424, $2.50.

Carlisle, Lilian Baker, **Pieced Work and Applique Quilts at Shelburne Museum**, Museum Pamphlet Series, No. 2, The Shelburne Museum, Shelburne, Vermont, 1957.

Christie, Archibald H., **Pattern Design; An Introduction to the Study of Formal Ornament**, Dover Publications, Inc., New York, 1969.

Clarke, Arthur C., "I'll Put a Girdle Around the Earth in 40 Minutes", **American Heritage**, October 1958, p. 40ff.

Colby, Averil, **Quilting**, Charles Scribner's Sons, New York 1971.

------**Patchwork**, B. T. Batsford Ltd., London and Charles T. Branford Co., Newton Centre, Mass., 1958.

Conroy, Mary, **Three Hundred Years of Canada's Quilts**, Griffen House, Toronto, 1976.

Dubois, Jean, **A Galaxy of Stars: America's Favorite Quilts**, La Plata Press, Durango, Colorado, 1976.

------"The Crazy Quilt-a Collage in Cloth", **Design**, Fall 1975.

Earle, Alice Morse, **Home Life in Colonial Days**, The Macmillan Company, New York, 1913.

Finley, Ruth, **Old Patchwork Quilts and the Women Who Made Them**, Charles T. Branford Company, Newton Centre, Massachusetts, 1929.

FitzRandolph, Mavis and Florence M. Fletcher, **Quilting: Traditional Methods and Design**, the Dryad Press, Leicester, 1968.

Gutcheon, Beth and Jeffrey, **The Quilt Design Workbook**, Rawson Associates Publishers, Inc., New York, 1976.

Haight, Ernest B., **Practical Machine-quilting for the Homemaker**, available by mail RFD #1, David City, Nebraska 68632, $1.35, no date.

Hake, Elizabeth, **English Quilting Old and New**, Charles Scribner's Sons, New York, B. T. Batsford Ltd., London, 1937.

Hale, Doris, "What Quilt Filling to Use?", **Better Homes and Gardens**, April, 1934, p. 81.

Hall, Carrie A. and Rose G. Kretsinger, **The Romance of the Patchwork Quilt in America**, Caxton Printers Ltd., Caldwell, Idaho, 1935.

Haywood, Dixie, **The Contemporary Crazy Quilt Project Book**, Crown Publishers Inc., New York, 1977

Holstein, Jonathan, **The Pieced Quilt, an American Design Tradition**, New York Graphic Society Ltd., Greenwich, Connecticut, 1973

Janos, Barbara S., "Amish Quilts", **American Collector**, January 1977, p. 15.

Leman, Bonnie, **Quick and Easy Quilting**, Hearthside Press Inc., Great Neck, New York, 1972.

Leman Publications, Inc., **Quilter's Newsletter Magazine**, Wheatridge, Colorado.

McKim, Ruby, **One Hundred and One Patchwork Patterns**, Dover Publications, Inc., New York, 1962.

Newman, Thelma R., **Quilting, Patchwork, Applique, and Trapunto, Traditional Methods and Original Designs,** Crown Publishers Inc. New York, 1974.

Orlofsky, Patsy and Myron, **Quilts in America**, McGraw-Hill Book Company, New York, 1974.

Renshaw, Donna, **Quilting-a Revived Art**, Los Altos, California, no date.

Safford, Carleton L. and Robert Bishop, **America's Quilts and Coverlets**, Weathervane Books, New York, 1974.

Shogren, Linda, **The Log Cabin Compendium**, 566 30th Ave., San Mateo, California 94403. 1977, $1.50 prepaid.

Tunis, Edwin, **Colonial Living**. The World Publishing Company, Cleveland and New York, 1957.

Wooster, Ann-Sargent, **Quiltmaking: The Modern Approach to a Traditional Craft**, Drake Publishers, Inc., New York, 1977.

INDEX